CASE STUDIES IN
21ST CENTURY SCHOOL ADMINISTRATION

CASE STUDIES IN 21ST CENTURY SCHOOL ADMINISTRATION

Addressing Challenges for Educational Leadership

David L. Gray
University of South Alabama

Agnes E. Smith
University of South Alabama

SAGE Publications
Thousand Oaks ▪ London ▪ New Delhi

For information:

Sage Publications, Inc.
2455 Teller Road
Thousand Oaks, California 91320
E-mail: order@sagepub.com

Sage Publications Ltd.
1 Oliver's Yard
55 City Road
London EC1Y 1SP
United Kingdom

Sage Publications India Pvt. Ltd.
B-42, Panchsheel Enclave
Post Box 4109
New Delhi 110 017 India

Printed in the United States of America

Library of Congress Cataloging-in-Publication Data

Gray, David L., 1948–
Case studies in 21st century school administration: Addressing challenges
for educational leadership / David L. Gray, Agnes E. Smith.
    p. cm.
Includes bibliographical references and index.
ISBN-13: 978-1-4129-2752-9 (cloth: alk. paper)
ISBN-13: 978-1-4129-2753-6 (pbk.: alk. paper)
   1. School management and organization—Case studies. 2. School administrators—Training of. I. Smith, Agnes E., 1949– II. Title. III. Title: Case studies in twenty-first century school administration.

LB2805.G684 2007
371.2—dc22   2006028263

This book is printed on acid-free paper.

07   08   09   10   11   10   9   8   7   6   5   4   3   2   1

Acquisitions Editor:	Diane McDaniel
Associate Editor:	Elise Smith
Editorial Assistant:	Ashley Plummer
Production Editor:	Diane S. Foster
Copy Editor:	Betty Pessagno
Typesetter:	C&M Digitals (P) Ltd.
Proofreader:	Scott Oney
Indexer:	Molly Hall
Cover Designer:	Janet Foulger

Contents

Preface

This text is written for students who plan to become school leaders. It contains case studies that are designed to enhance their analytical skills and to develop their problem-solving abilities because those are the skills administrators need to be effective in their jobs.

Each case in the text is based on the authors' experiences during 30 years as principals and represents a microcosm of the issues with which school leaders contend. Readers may think the behaviors of some of the parents, teachers, students, and administrators in the text to be unusual, but *these cases really happened!*

After teaching aspiring school leaders for a decade, we have discovered a few truths about people who want to lead. First, without making the emotional, mental, and physical commitment to leadership that motivates a principal, the majority of teachers who aspire to that position have only a vague idea of what the job entails. Some of them are sincere about wanting to improve learning conditions for students; others see advancement as a pathway to a higher salary.

Second, we try to convince tomorrow's administrators that communication is both art and science. Their mastery of its complexities is requisite to successful leadership. Those who understand that language skills are paramount in the business of working with students, teachers, and other stakeholders have a greater chance at success.

Third, effective leaders find ways to empower the people around them. They care that others are striving toward worthy goals, and they look for opportunities to reward accomplishment. The day of the principal as an autocratic leader is gone. A new paradigm of leading successful learning organizations is based on collaboration and collegial relations.

We hope that professors and students of educational leadership who read this text will immerse themselves in the details of school administration. Our cases are complex and require thoughtful analysis. Students are advised to remember that a problem's solution is not always obvious at first glance.

MAKING DECISIONS

Principals make hundreds of job-related decisions every day. Many of them are routine and only require knowledge of current policies and procedures, but others test the limits of what a leader can be expected to know. As an example, what should a principal do about teachers whose students detract from the school's efforts to make Annual Yearly Progress on a standardized test? Important legal and ethical issues are entwined within that question.

There is an answer; it lies in the code of behavior that administrators should use to guide their actions when faced with challenges. In 1996 the Council of Chief State School Officers published the Interstate School Leaders Licensure Consortium (ISLLC) Standards to help school leaders understand the professional responsibilities for which they are accountable. Each standard is supported with knowledge, disposition, and performance requirements that should be used to shape a principal's perspective about leadership during periods of reflection and self-assessment.

—David L. Gray and Agnes E. Smith
The University of South Alabama
Mobile, Alabama

Acknowledgments

We would like to thank the reviewers whose feedback helped us shape this book so that it will best serve the needs of students and instructors:

Michael J. Anderson, University of Texas at Arlington

John J. Battles, George Washington University

Cozette M. Buckney, Roosevelt University

Rodney Davis, Troy University Dothan Campus

Roger C. Shouse, Penn State

Olusegun A. Sogunro, Central Connecticut State University

Karen L. Stevens, Tennessee State University

A Guide to Using Case Studies

Using case studies as a problem-solving forum is a recent phenomenon in educational administration. Traditionally, aspiring administrators received an essential curriculum of law, finance, and courses centered on leadership theories, traits, and principles. They were expected to acquire interpersonal relationship skills and technical competence through on-the-job training after their first leadership appointment.

Times have changed. The No Child Left Behind Act requires teachers to be highly qualified and schools to make Annual Yearly Progress on high-stakes testing. Principals do not have time to make a gentle transition from graduate classes to school leadership. Only a few administrative interns have participated in field experiences in which they could observe firsthand what principals really do, but they come, armed with theory, to lead and improve student learning.

Case studies offer opportunities to learn from experienced professionals. They also give aspiring principals an idea of the spectrum of challenges they will encounter. A unique feature of school leadership is that many of its difficult moments take place behind closed doors and away from the faculty's eyes and ears. If teachers are unaware of a problem in the office, they do not assume that one has occurred. The principal stands at the center of a storm, trying to use available resources to improve the learning environment for students and staff.

We suggest that readers will benefit most from their case study experience if they read the case carefully and completely without judging the people involved until the class has discussed all pertinent issues. Readers should

- Evaluate the case with regard to the school's organizational structure. Large schools tend to use a bureaucratic approach to problem solving more often than small schools do.

- Identify the central issue within the case study. Administrators deal with complex challenges and must be able to isolate key elements from those of lesser importance. Communication skills are vital to this process.
- Make a list of the issues in each case that are important to address and assign a relative value to each of them. Reflection and analysis will enable one to spend one's time with the most important challenges.
- Use the list from the previous step to identify possible solutions to the issues described there and consider all possibilities. Sometimes the best solution to a problem comes from combining several alternatives.
- Weigh the probable outcomes of implementing the course of action favored and consider how to assess the effects of that decision.

Each of our case studies offers the reader a **Background** of relevant facts and issues that influence the case. **Factors to Consider** are broad areas of responsibility that shape a school administrator's daily routine and are beacons for case issues. **The Case** describes the actions and activities of people in school that require attention and will test aspiring administrators' leadership skills.

Each case is followed by **Questions** to guide students toward research-based solutions to the problems they have identified. **Interstate School Leaders Licensure Consortium Standards** (ISLLC) (1996), complete with associated Knowledge, Disposition, and Performance requirements, point to "significant trends in society and education that hold implications for emerging views of leadership—and subsequently for the standards that give meaning to those new perspectives on leadership" (p. 5). Each of the standards warrants thorough discussion and understanding by prospective school leaders.

Finally, the authors recommend that leadership students engage in the **Activities** at the end of each case. Many of them entail role-playing so that students might experience the case's complexity from different perspectives. Each case includes a provision for a written exercise. Our experience as principals and professors leads us to believe that graduate students must have impeccable writing skills as part of a larger communicative talent, and they must learn to write concisely.

Nothing can substitute for *being* a school leader. Graduate classes stimulate your thinking, but the emotional and physical investment of your resources is aimed at earning good grades and a degree. Leading others and taking ownership for the successes and failures of *your* school is another matter. We hope our text helps with the transition.

A Matrix of Case Studies

Case Number	Title	Organization	Primary Issue	Secondary Issue	ISLLC Standard
1	Teacher's Absences Create Problems	Secondary	Supervising staff	Conflict management	2, 3
2	A Good Teacher Turns Bad	Elementary	Evaluating teachers	Instructional leadership	1
3	Experienced Teachers Need Clear Expectations, Too!	Elementary	Faculty morale	Supervising instruction	3, 4
4	Grandmother's Medicine	Elementary	Student safety	Legal issues	3
5	Is Dismissal Justified?	Secondary	Suspected immoral teacher behavior	Human resources procedures	2, 3
6	School Property Is Missing	Secondary	Managing financial resources	Legal issues	5
7	Who Has the Missing Crayons?	Elementary	Student search and seizure	Conflict management	3, 4, 5
8	A Good Student Earns Detention	Elementary	Assessing pupil performance	Instructional leadership	2, 5
9	Copyright and the Computer	Secondary	Budget development	Managing resources	5, 6

(Continued)

(Continued)

Case Number	Title	Organization	Primary Issue	Secondary Issue	ISLLC Standard
10	Too Much Parent Involvement!	Elementary	Conflict management	Parent conferences	3, 4
11	Double Promotion?	Elementary	Instructional leadership	Student achievement	2, 5
12	A Problem With Inclusion	Secondary	Parent involvement	Special education	3, 6
13	Poor Evaluations for a Teacher	Elementary	Evaluation of teachers	Professional development	5, 6
14	Missing Booster Club Funds	Secondary	Collaborating with parent groups	Parent participation in the school	3, 4
15	Mentoring New Teachers	Elementary	Communication	Faculty morale	2, 3
16	A Gift for the Principal	Secondary	Leadership ethics	Financial management	3, 5
17	Unprofessional Behavior	Secondary	Professional behavior	Ethical behavior	1, 2
18	It All Depends on the Numbers	Secondary	Data-driven instruction	Instructional leadership	5, 6
19	All A's Are Not Enough	Secondary	Conflict management	Leadership of extracurricular activities	1, 5
20	The Community Won't Understand	Elementary	Alternative lifestyles	Personnel management	4, 5
21	Every Day Counts!	Secondary	Attendance policies	Student achievement	1, 2
22	Illegal Drugs at School	Secondary	Disciplinary violations	Student discipline	3, 4
23	Internet Use Violations	Secondary	Student rights	Teacher competence	5, 6

CASE 1

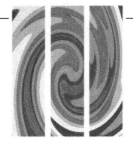

A Teacher's Absences Create Problems

Holding Teachers Accountable for Excessive Absences

Experience and observation suggest that one of the most important ways in which teachers teach is by example. Teachers who begin instruction promptly each day or each class period communicate a strong message to their students. Such teachers reinforce the importance of using time wisely and the significance of daily instructional goals and objectives. They also facilitate the development of a clear focus on academic achievement and learning among students. The consistent presence of the teacher sets the tone for students to value productivity in the classroom. Moreover, students grow to understand that the teacher genuinely cares about them and their academic progress. Effective teachers communicate the importance of instruction by beginning classes on time and by being present unless they are scheduled for professional development opportunities or they are experiencing illness or emergencies. Through their presence, planning, and lesson delivery, highly effective teachers communicate to students that the work they are doing is important. Students learn from their teachers' example of dedication and commitment to be prompt and to approach learning with a similar dedication.

Teachers' requests for leave are governed by local school policies. Teachers are required to be on duty a specified number of days prior to the opening of school and to remain on duty a specified number of days after the last day of school for students. On the days when students are in attendance, teachers are required to be on duty unless appropriate leave is approved at the local school and central office levels or unless the teacher's reason for being absent relates to an emergency or family or personal illness. While school districts allow a certain number of days for sick leave, typically one day a month, teachers who are absent for an extended period of time due to illness or any other personal or professional reason must either receive school board approval to be absent or provide appropriate documentation that satisfies requirements of local school district personnel policy.

Special provisions must be made when a teacher is pregnant and another teacher will be needed to assume interim responsibilities for the time the regular teacher is on maternity leave. When teachers attend professional development in-service meetings or conferences, provisions must be made for their absences. Furthermore, when teachers are absent for reasons of illness or emergency, a substitute must be secured to conduct daily activities with students. It is the school principal's responsibility to communicate to teachers a consistent method of preparing for substitutes. Some principals require teachers to follow a specific lesson plan format when absent, whereas other principals might request that teachers develop a folder of grade-level or subject matter activities to guide the classroom work for the term of absence.

Because of the relationship between teacher attendance and student productivity, principals need to be prepared to respond to parents' and teacher colleagues' concerns when a teacher must take extended leave. While parents' concerns will understandably focus on the consistency of their children's instructional program, department and grade-level teachers will be worried about "taking up the slack" until the regular teacher has returned to school. Clear communication to all interested parties is necessary to avoid misunderstandings and provide reassurance. When a teacher and principal have prior knowledge of an extended absence, policies can be reviewed, preparations made, and communications issued for parents and other vested parties. However, when frequent or extended absences occur on a day-to-day basis, adherence to personnel policies and procedures becomes even more important for principals.

When a teacher begins to develop a pattern of excessive absenteeism, a principal must balance the needs of the teacher and school allowances for absences with the need to have a certified, competent teacher working with students on a consistent basis. Many factors have to be weighed. What is the reason for the teacher's absence(s)? Is the teacher absent for successive days, or is there a pattern of sporadic absences? How many years of experience does the teacher have? If the teacher is experienced or tenured, what is his or her past performance history? Has the teacher provided materials and lesson plans for a substitute that will provide productive activities for students? Is it possible to secure the services of a regular substitute who is already familiar with school routines and schedules?

FACTORS TO CONSIDER

- Adherence to local school district personnel policies/procedures
- Provision of a consistent, quality instructional program
- Public relations with parents, community members
- Legal dimensions of teacher performance evaluation
- Communication and organizational conflict

THE CASE

Mr. Samuel Taylor is principal of Walnut Creek K–8 School. Walnut Creek serves 750 students from kindergarten through eighth grade. Only three years ago, the school served the same grade levels with a student population of 527. Because of new industry that has moved into the area, the suburb in which the school is located is experiencing rapid growth and demands for housing. The location of the Walnut Creek community is also attractive, because it is only an hour's drive from the coast and pristine beaches for vacation activities. Parents have told Mr. Taylor that they appreciate the opportunity to have their children enrolled in the same school for nine years and to live in an area that offers access to the coast.

Because of the population growth in the Walnut Creek community, the school gained three new teacher units for this academic year—one at the kindergarten level, one for fourth grade, and an additional physical education teacher. Mr. Taylor was able to interview and recommend applicants for the kindergarten and physical education positions prior to the opening of school. Because the increase in student population at the fourth grade level was not expected, he had fewer applicants from which to choose to fill the new fourth grade position, and the assistant superintendent of human resources asked him to consider recommending a young teacher, Mrs. Green, whose husband was appointed assistant coach at the nearby high school. After an interview with the teacher and a review of her reference letters, Mr. Taylor honored the assistant superintendent of human resources' request and recommended that Mrs. Green be appointed as fourth grade teacher for this new teaching position.

At first, Mrs. Green seemed to make efforts to be friendly with other teachers and to meet the duties and responsibilities of the job. For the first four weeks of school, she was present every day, and she arrived for early-morning duty on time, except for one occasion when she apologized for oversleeping. Then during the fifth week of school, she called in sick on Friday. This absence was the beginning of a pattern that became apparent by Christmas. Mrs. Green called in sick on the first Friday of every month from September through December. School board policy governing teacher sick days reads as follows:

> Full-time employees receive one accumulated sick day for each month worked. Continued unpaid absences are unacceptable and may result in disciplinary action up to and including termination.

At the Christmas break, Mrs. Green had used all of her sick leave days and had none to carry over after the holidays.

Two weeks after Christmas, Mrs. Green's three-year old son was hospitalized for a week, and she called Mr. Taylor to tell him that she needed to be with her son. Mr. Taylor expressed concern for Mrs. Green's son. He explained that because she had no accumulated sick leave days, she would need a doctor's statement; otherwise her absence would be considered neglect of her duties. The day she returned to school, Mrs. Green gave Mr. Taylor a statement from her son's pediatrician supporting her need to stay in the hospital with her son. When Mr. Taylor submitted the weekly personnel report to the district's Department of Human Resources, he attached the doctor's statement to it. According to policy, Mrs. Green's absences due to the illness of her son were excused, but her salary was reduced by the number of days absent.

During Mrs. Green's week-long absence, parents of two students in her class asked to see Mr. Taylor. The parents, Mrs. Gray and Mrs. Williams, expressed concern about Mrs. Green's extended absence from the classroom.

"I understand her son is ill, Mr. Taylor," said Mrs. Gray, "but our children are falling behind the other fourth grade classes in English and math. We're worried about the SAT tests that our children will take in April. If they continue to fall behind, they won't do well."

Mr. Taylor listened to the parents' concerns. He expressed appreciation for their patience, and he commented that he knew they understood the need for a mother to be with her small child in the hospital. He assured them that Mrs. Green's son was well and that she was working diligently to ensure that her students were as prepared for standardized testing as all the other fourth grade students.

As the parents left Mr. Taylor's office, Mrs. Williams stated, "We appreciate your time, Mr. Taylor, and we do understand Mrs. Green's need to care for her preschool-age son. However, now that he is well, we expect our children to have full-time, uninterrupted instruction for the remainder of the school year!"

Mr. Taylor thoughtfully considered options for working with Mrs. Green and her absences from the classroom. He reviewed the school board policy for teachers' sick leave and turned to his computer keyboard to develop the following memo to Mrs. Green.

MEMO: Mrs. Green

FROM: Mr. Taylor

RE: Extended Absences from School

I want you to know that I appreciate your need to care for your preschool son during his recent hospital stay for a serious case of influenza. However, I want to bring the school board policy regarding teacher sick leave days to your attention.

   Because you were absent four Fridays of school prior to the Christmas holidays, you had no sick leave days to support your absence when your son was in the hospital. Your personnel record reflects nine days of absence from school since September, five of which were unpaid days of sick leave. According to school board policy, additional sick leave days will subject you to disciplinary action up to and including termination. Please let me know if you have questions regarding this policy or its application to your situation. I will be available to conference with you tomorrow or another day this week.

Mr. Taylor placed the memo in a sealed envelope in Mrs. Green's office mailbox. He watched that afternoon as she collected her mail from her mailbox. He witnessed Mrs. Green taking the envelope from her mailbox with other announcements and mail. Although Mr. Taylor was available to see Mrs. Green each day for the remainder of the week, she didn't request a conference to discuss the status of her sick leave personnel record.

During the first week in February, Mr. Taylor distributed a memo to all teachers requesting dates for scheduled observations. The evaluation process for teachers requires a minimum of two observations for every teacher each year. While one observation may be unannounced, a second must be scheduled at a time convenient to the administrator and known by the teacher. Mr. Taylor had completed all unannounced observations of teachers, including Mrs. Green, before Christmas. When Mr. Taylor observed Mrs. Green's teaching in November, he documented her performance during a social studies lesson. Mr. Taylor commented that Mrs. Green's objective was clear and that she used both visual and auditory lesson delivery techniques. He recommended that she consider a structured way to evaluate students' progress with lesson objectives. He noted that she reviewed the written assignment of only 14 of her 25 students. The other 11 students received no feedback from Mrs. Green.

By the end of February, Mrs. Green had not requested a date for her scheduled observation. Mr. Taylor made a mental note to speak with her on the last Friday of the month, but she called in sick on that day. Before the end of the Friday of her absence, a fourth grade colleague, Mrs. Matthews, came to the office during her planning time to speak to Mr. Taylor.

"I think you should know, Mr. Taylor, that Mrs. Green told me yesterday that her dad, who is a state legislator, has a condominium at the beach. In fact," Mrs. Matthews added, "Mrs. Green told me that her father has made his condominium available to her husband and her during the months of February through April. She boasted to all fourth grade teachers yesterday that her father is politically influential because he serves on the state finance and homeland legislative committees. I just thought you'd like to be apprised of her attitude, Mr. Taylor. The other fourth grade teachers are upset that she considers her absences from school to be of little consequence."

Mr. Taylor gave some thought to Mrs. Matthews's statements and prepared another memo for Mrs. Green, which read:

MEMO: Mrs. Green

FROM: Mr. Taylor

RE: Sick Leave Days

Please see me during your planning time the day you return to school. We need to discuss the school board sick leave policy as well as the teacher evaluation process. I asked you the first of February to let me know a day for a scheduled observation. One month has gone by, and I haven't received notice from you about a date for this observation.

Mrs. Green came to Mr. Taylor's office the Monday she returned to school as requested. When Mr. Taylor asked Mrs. Green to explain her absence the previous Friday, she told him that she had personal business. Mr. Taylor explained that because she didn't receive prior approval for this absence and because she had no proof of an emergency or medical reason for the absence, it would be considered unexcused unpaid leave.

The conference did not go well. Mrs. Green responded defensively to Mr. Taylor's comments. She stated that she didn't receive the memo about scheduling an announced observation and that she was offended that her reasons for being absent were questioned. Mrs. Green stood abruptly and moved to the door. As she reached for the doorknob, she turned to Mr. Taylor and said, "I have nothing further to say, Mr. Taylor, until I speak with the local teachers' association director, who is a friend of my dad's. I can assure you that he'll be asking for documentation that other teachers are required to submit doctor's excuses or request prior approval for their absences!"

Questions

1. In what ways and when should school district policies be communicated to school personnel?

2. What is the most effective way to address the problem of frequent absences with Mrs. Green?

3. Are there other personnel at the central office level who need to be involved in resolving this problem?

4. What provisions should be made for a consistent instructional program for students if a teacher needs to be absent for an extended period?

5. Will you decide to recommend termination for the teacher or plan to renew her contract?

Activities

1. Draft a memo to Mrs. Green that documents and addresses your concern about her frequent absences.

2. Role-play a conference with the teacher about her absences.

3. Role-play a conference with a parent who complains about the teacher's absences.

4. Develop professional development goals for the teacher to meet by the end of the evaluation period.

5. Outline the points you will address with the teacher at an end-of-the-year conference in which you (a) recommend contract renewal or (b) recommend contract termination.

ISLLC Standards

STANDARD 2—A school administrator is an educational leader who promotes the success of all students by advocating, nurturing, and sustaining a school culture and instructional program conducive to student learning and staff professional growth.

Knowledge

The administrator has knowledge and understanding of:

- Principles of effective instruction
- Student growth and development
- School cultures

Dispositions

The administrator believes in, values, and is committed to:

- Student learning as the fundamental purpose of schooling
- A safe and supportive learning environment

Performances

The administrator facilitates processes and engages in activities ensuring that:

- All individuals are treated with fairness, dignity, and respect
- Students and staff feel valued and important
- There is a culture of high expectations for self, student, and staff performance
- The school culture and climate are assessed on a regular basis

---

STANDARD 3—A school administrator is an educational leader who promotes the success of all students by ensuring management of the organization, operations, and resources for a safe, efficient, and effective learning environment.

Knowledge

The administrator has knowledge and understanding of:

- Operational procedures at the school and district level
- Human resources management and development
- Legal issues impacting school operations

Dispositions

The administrator believes in, values, and is committed to:

- Making management decisions to enhance learning and teaching
- High-quality standards, expectations, and performances

Performances

The administrator facilitates processes and engages in activities, ensuring that:

- Knowledge of learning, teaching, and student development is used to inform management decisions
- Operational procedures are designed and managed to maximize opportunities for successful learning
- Time is managed to maximize attainment of organizational goals

CASE 2

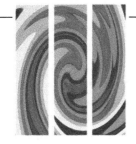

A Good Teacher Turns Bad

Stress at Home Creates Problems at School

Marsh and Willis (2003) have summarized research on leadership styles and reported that principals lead as *initiators, responders,* or *managers.* Initiators are forward-looking, anticipatory, and aggressive about improving learning conditions in their schools. Responders are cautious, inclined to wait until all risks are identified before making decisions, and less likely to take risks. Managers are more interested in procedures and systems than people.

New administrators realize soon enough that their perspective on leadership changes after several years of experience. The complexity of interpersonal relationships demands competence in skills that cannot be taught in graduate classes, and effective leaders learn to adapt their style to situational requirements. School problems are real, not simulated. A principal's values are reflected through interactions with the school's stakeholders, and especially with faculty.

Leadership is a daunting challenge. Think about your first faculty. They're waiting for you. A number of them will have more experience than you at teaching. They helped to create the culture of the school, and you'll have to prove your competence to earn their trust.

Others view administrators with a wary eye. They prefer to be left alone in their classrooms to teach children, and they rely on you to shield them from the incessant barrage of rules, regulations, and reports in which administrators seem to revel.

Several others are ready to retire but can't afford to stop working. They've lost their zeal for teaching but don't know what else to do with their lives. What will you do to guide them in the right direction?

Probationary teachers are the most fragile faculty. They haven't yet earned continuing service status (tenure). Two of five probationary teachers will leave teaching within two years. Another one will remain through the fourth or fifth year, then seek a different career to earn more money and because working with children wasn't fulfilling. How will you retain teachers in whom your district has already made a considerable financial investment? You'll define your leadership style through interactions with faculty.

FACTORS TO CONSIDER

- School district personnel policies
- Student safety
- Documenting employee misconduct
- Faculty morale
- Communication skills

THE CASE

Crestview Elementary School is located in a rural area and is one of three elementary schools in the district. Jean Wilson's assignment as principal of Crestview came after 13 years of teaching and four years of night classes at the university to earn an administrative certificate.

The faculty consists of 18 classroom teachers, a media center specialist, a counselor, two special education teachers, and three aides. They have worked together for eight years and are proud of the school and their students' accomplishments.

Mrs. Wilson was cautious about change during her first year, recalling a professor's advice about not "rocking the boat," as he was accustomed to saying. There didn't seem to be much to change, anyway. Attendance was good, test scores were above average, and parents in the community were pleased with the school.

Soon after spring break in her third year, Mrs. Wilson noticed something different in the attitude and behavior of Mrs. Horton, a first grade teacher, former Teacher of the Year in the district, and a seasoned professional. She seemed stressed and less friendly than before. She argued with other teachers and became upset when anyone disagreed with her suggestions.

Mrs. Wilson learned from Mrs. Horton's colleagues that she was having a rough time at home. Mrs. Horton's husband had moved out, leaving her to raise their two teen-aged sons on her own. The end of the school year arrived without incident, and the principal hoped that the teacher's difficulties would be resolved during the break.

The summer was uneventful as Mrs. Wilson prepared to open school the next year. Mrs. Horton, who frequently came to school during vacations and holidays to work in her classroom, was conspicuously absent. Perhaps she hadn't been able to work through her problems, the principal decided.

The school year began in a positive way. Crestview was chosen to pilot a new reading program that Mrs. Wilson and many of her faculty supported. Unfortunately, Mrs. Horton disagreed with the decision to change programs and berated the teachers who favored it. A private conference with Mrs. Horton did nothing to discourage her.

The principal began to receive phone calls and letters about Mrs. Horton within the first six weeks of the year. Parents reported that she was verbally abusive to their children during class, screamed at children who made mistakes, was late arriving at school several days each week, and refused to hold parent-teacher conferences. Mrs. Wilson's strong affirmation that she had visited the first grade teacher's classroom regularly during the past few weeks and found no evidence of abusive behavior failed to reassure them.

The superintendent telephoned to inform Mrs. Wilson that four parents had called board of education members to complain about Mrs. Horton's behavior and to demand that their children be reassigned to another first grade teacher. Mrs. Wilson promised to investigate further.

She decided to confront Mrs. Horton with these mounting concerns and dissatisfaction about her professional behavior when Mr. Stafford, the father of one of her students, arrived at school and insisted on a conference with the principal. He insisted that his daughter, Julie, should be moved out of "that woman's" room immediately. "Julie cries every morning before school and is having difficulty sleeping and eating," he complained. Mrs. Horton had ignored his wife's notes and telephone calls asking for a conference, and he refused to put his daughter through another day of torture!

Mrs. Wilson promised to arrange a parent-teacher meeting and agreed to attend, but she would not promise to move his daughter to another room until the conference had taken place. The principal visited Mrs. Horton's room that afternoon after the children had been dismissed and told her about the phone calls and letters she had received, as well as about Mr. Stafford's visit earlier in the day. Though defensive, Mrs. Horton agreed to the conference planned for the next morning.

The next day Mr. Stafford arrived ahead of time. Mrs. Wilson escorted him to Mrs. Horton's room, still hoping to resolve his frustration with Mrs. Horton and to restore his confidence in her teaching ability. The teacher greeted the parent and principal warmly at the door and invited them to sit at her conference table. The chairs were first grade size and uncomfortable. Mrs. Horton excused herself to rummage through her desk for a grade book and examples of Julie's work. Mr. Stafford became angry. He had taken several hours away from work and didn't plan to spend time waiting for Mrs. Horton to prepare herself for the meeting.

Mrs. Wilson began the meeting by stating its purpose and asking Mr. Stafford what he hoped its outcome would be. "My wife and I want Julie out of Mrs. Horton's room."

Mrs. Wilson then asked for an explanation.

"She upsets the children," he replied. "She screams at them all day and embarrasses them in front of . . ."

"You're a liar!" Mrs. Horton shouted, slamming her hand onto the table. "Those are lies! Every one of them!" Her face was red with anger and her co-verbal behavior was confrontational.

Mr. Stafford, taken aback by Mrs. Horton's interruption, looked at the principal for help.

"I think it would be better if we postponed this meeting," Mrs. Wilson said as she stood and extended a hand to her visitor. "Mr. Stafford, I'll call you later to talk about this. I know you want a decision about Julie as quickly as possible, but Mrs. Horton and I need to discuss this situation in more detail."

Mr. Stafford shook her hand and walked to the door, accepting the principal's assurance that Julie's placement would receive immediate attention.

"Just think what the children go through in here every day," he said as he closed the door. Stunned by Mrs. Horton's outburst, Mrs. Wilson turned to her for an explanation. Mrs. Horton was still angry and her posture was defensive.

Questions

1. What will Mrs. Wilson say to Mrs. Horton?

2. Will the principal reassign Julie to another first grade teacher? If she does, what are the consequences of that decision?

3. Should documentation of this incident become part of Mrs. Horton's personnel file? If so, in what format? What are the principal's legal responsibilities to her?

4. What will Mrs. Wilson say to Mr. Stafford?

Activities

1. Role-play the conference between Mr. Stafford, Mrs. Horton, and the principal. Afterward, discuss each person's perspective about reasons for the meeting and its outcome.

2. Write a memorandum to Mrs. Horton expressing your opinion (as the principal) about her conduct at the outset of the conference. What elements should be included in the memo? Will you talk with her about the document?

3. What will Mrs. Wilson tell other parents who complain about Mrs. Horton and want their children reassigned to another classroom? Should the principal discuss this incident with other faculty? If so, with whom?

4. What steps should Mrs. Wilson take to help Mrs. Horton?

ISLLC Standards

STANDARD 1—A school administrator is an educational leader who promotes the success of all students by facilitating the development, articulation, implementation, and stewardship of a vision of learning that is shared and supported by the school community.

Knowledge

The administrator has knowledge and understanding of:

- Effective communication
- Effective consensus-building and negotiation skills

Dispositions

The administrator believes in, values, and is committed to:

- A willingness to continuously examine one's own assumptions, beliefs, and practices
- Doing the work required for high levels of personal and organization performance

Performances

The administrator facilitates processes and engages in activities ensuring that:

- Barriers to achieving the vision are identified, clarified, and addressed
- Existing resources are used in support of the school vision and goals

REFERENCE

Marsh, C. J., & Willis, G. (2003). *Curriculum: Alternative approaches, ongoing issues* (3rd ed.). Upper Saddle River, NJ: Pearson Education.

CASE 3

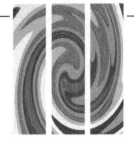

Experienced Teachers Need Clear Expectations, Too

Handling Conflicts With Practiced Educators

Personnel issues are among the toughest that school principals face. As middle management executives, they are called upon to resolve problems, settle disputes, motivate professional and classified employees, and listen to the concerns, complaints, and worries of others. Moreover, principals are responsible for setting the tone for their schools. In an effective school, the focus is on student learning. All aspects of the school program and facility are organized, scheduled, and arranged to provide optimum conditions for student achievement. Smith and Andrews (1989) describe one of the competencies of leadership as "management of attention . . . the leader's ability to get teachers to focus and expand their energies toward fulfilling the purpose of school" (p. 5). The ultimate goal of the principal is to have teachers make full use of instructional time with students engaged in productive learning activities.

Principals communicate expectations to teachers in many ways. When teachers are new to a school, an orientation session for new teachers is a quick and efficient way for a principal to talk about many aspects of the school, the community, and the principal's expectations of them. If teachers are more experienced, principals are able to influence their performance by planning professional development opportunities. It's important that principals involve teachers in planning professional development, either through a leadership team or committee or through a survey about topics of interest to teachers.

Needs identified through the teacher evaluation process may be included in topics offered for professional development.

Another technique that principals can use to communicate expectations and to motivate teachers to be highly effective is to circulate memos or a regularly published newsletter that describes innovative, varied teaching techniques. Teachers may be encouraged to contribute their own ideas to this newsletter. Effective techniques, new ideas, and innovative approaches to instruction can be shared by teachers on grade-level or subject matter areas. Through the use of such a publication, a principal may be described as a strong instructional leader.

Moreover, faculty meeting time may be highly productive when principals include a demonstration of a new curricular program, updated materials, or emerging technologies. Faculty meetings become more than just a time to share information about routines and upcoming events. Rather, they become an important time for teachers to be inspired to try new and different ways to organize and deliver instruction.

Principals who value their role as instructional leaders use brief visits to classrooms, the formal teacher evaluation process required by their school districts, and anecdotal comments from parents and/or other teachers to identify areas where their teachers need to improve. When principals schedule a walk-through of classrooms on a daily basis, they are able to observe teachers at work during different times of the day as well as when students are receiving instruction in different subjects or class periods. Despite the brevity of each classroom visit, experienced principals can note the students' level of engagement, the teacher's skills in classroom management, and the variety of instructional techniques used by the teacher.

Moreover, principals learn to rely on school district and local school policies to enhance the instructional program offered to students in the school. By serving on district-level committees, principals can provide input into locally developed curriculum guides, procedures, and classroom schedule development. Although most state departments of education govern the number of minutes allocated for instruction in different subject matter areas, local districts sometimes formulate policies that require additional attention to specialized areas of instruction or that define parameters for the use of media such as videos or DVDs.

Wise principals will work with teachers to develop local school policies and procedures for the use of library materials and media equipment. After these policies are developed, they should be communicated to teachers via e-mail, a teacher handbook, or an individual handout. It is appropriate for a principal to review policies with teachers at the beginning of a school year and to invite discussion in case changes in the policies are warranted. A key person in the development of policies regarding the use of library materials and media equipment is the school library/media specialist. The library/media specialist's training and preparation will offer teachers the most current knowledge about the productive use of instructional techniques enhanced through emerging technologies. Communicating information about the appropriate use of media materials and equipment will avoid overuse and nonproductive use of videos, DVDs, and computer programs.

Once teachers have a clear understanding of expectations with regard to use of media materials and equipment, principals must monitor and enforce compliance. It is at this point that the principal will rely on walk-throughs, planned as well as unannounced classroom observations, and review of teachers' lesson plans to assess whether or not they are using media materials and equipment to enhance lesson objectives or to entertain students while the teacher grades papers or attends to other clerical duties.

If a principal determines that a teacher relies on the use of videos or DVDs to entertain students instead of to fulfill valid instructional purposes, this concern needs to be addressed. Sometimes a general memo to all faculty and staff members is the best option to consider. Other times, however, if only one teacher's overuse of videos or DVDs is grossly inappropriate, a principal may need to directly address his or her concern with the offending teacher.

FACTORS TO CONSIDER

- Administrative responsibilities of a principal to serve as instructional leader of the school
- Development of local school policies that clearly communicate expectations to faculty and staff
- Instructional dimensions of teacher performance evaluations
- Communication and organizational structure
- Use of committees

THE CASE

Anita Parsons is a third-year principal of Midtown Elementary School. Once on the outskirts of a metropolitan area, as a result of incorporation measures and population growth the school is now in the middle of an inner-city area that has declined during the past 10 years. The school serves over 900 students in what is now an economically deprived area of the city. Although the school building is sound and with better landscaping could be considered attractive, the neighborhood consists of small, somewhat dilapidated older homes and two nightclubs that operate every weekday on a 24-hour basis. The nightclubs are visible from the second story of the school. Frequently, police are called to break up fights and deal with unruly customers. Fortunately, the police routinely patrol the street because of suspected drug use and drug sales in and around the nightclubs.

The student population of Midtown Elementary School reflects little diversity. All students are from homes of poverty, and most share similar cultural heritages. From time to time, students of different cultures enroll at Midtown Elementary. Their enculturation into the student population is unstrained, as all students deal with similar challenges owing to their families' low socioeconomic status.

When Mrs. Parsons was first appointed to Midtown Elementary School as principal, the teacher turnover rate was high. More than 40 percent of the teachers requested transfers to other schools on an annual basis. Curbing this transfer request rate was a goal she set from her first day on the job. Teachers credit Mrs. Parsons's commitment to support them in their "mission" to teach in the community with reducing the transfer request rate to 20 percent in only two years. Despite the lower socioeconomic status of the community and the lack of parental support, Mrs. Parsons describes Midtown Elementary School as a school that offers all students a chance for a brighter future. She strengthens this message with teachers by explaining that their job is to practice exemplary teaching and use "every precious minute of instructional time productively."

One of the most helpful tools Mrs. Parsons developed for teacher support and communication is the Midtown Elementary Teachers' Handbook. Prior to her tenure at the school, teachers had no handbook. In addition to general policies and procedures, Mrs. Parsons developed a comprehensive section that described the characteristics of effective teachers and the qualities of a strong instructional program. At the beginning of every academic year, Mrs. Parsons conducts a new teacher orientation as an opportunity to focus on the instructional chapter of the teacher handbook. She takes time to discuss development of an effective lesson, use of instructional time, and appropriate use of audio-visual equipment and emerging technologies.

Because Midtown Elementary School is scheduled for a review by a regional accreditation agency in two years, Mrs. Parsons works with teachers to analyze a dated mission statement and list of common beliefs shared by the faculty. A committee of lead teachers developed a draft mission statement that was edited by the faculty at large. In September of this year, the current faculty voted to adopt the following mission statement: *The mission of this school is to provide students with instructional opportunities that prepare them for career development and success in future life.* The list of beliefs approved by teachers includes the following: Wise use of instructional time promotes productive learning experiences.

With help and support from the federal programs division of the local school district, Mrs. Parsons secured funding to purchase 24 computers for a computer lab, six VCR/DVD units and TV monitors, and two LCD projectors for use by teachers. The library/media specialist at Midtown, Mrs. Booker, conducts afternoon workshops about how to use this new equipment and related materials effectively for interested teachers. Mrs. Booker developed a calendar that allows teachers to sign up for use of available equipment on an as-needed basis. This sign-up procedure requires teachers to list at least one instructional objective that justifies use of the equipment. During the workshops, Mrs. Booker explains that teachers should limit their use of the computer lab to once a week, and their requests for video/DVD equipment to twice a week. To minimize movement of the LCD projectors, teachers are asked to bring their students to the audiovisual area of the library/media center.

While Mrs. Parsons was conducting a walk-through on the Friday following Mrs. Booker's workshops, Mrs. Booker asked her to look at the sign-up form for use of the VCR/DVD units and monitors. Mrs. Parsons was surprised by what she found. Mrs. McDavid, a third grade teacher, had signed up to use the VCR for two hours during every afternoon three weeks prior to the Christmas holidays. Mrs. Booker asked, "How should I handle this situation, Mrs. Parsons? Already other teachers are complaining about how Mrs. McDavid's actions have limited the availability of VCR/DVD units."

One of the disgruntled teachers used a red felt-tip pen to write the note, "You're hogging use of the VCR, Mrs. Mc!"

Mrs. Booker added, "Mrs. McDavid is the only teacher who chose not to attend the library/media workshops on the use of the new equipment."

Mrs. McDavid has been teaching at Midtown for 24 years. When Mrs. Parsons first came to work at Midtown Elementary, the school secretary, Mrs. Richardson, told her that Mrs. McDavid formerly was a favorite among parents. In recent years, her reputation has changed. She has come to be known as a teacher who yells at students and assigns a lot of nonproductive busywork. Mrs. Parsons has noticed that other teachers avoid Mrs. McDavid in the cafeteria. When Mrs. Parsons asked the secretary if she knew why, the secretary told her that Mrs. McDavid was recognized as a complainer among her peers. At the end of last year when Mrs. Parsons mentioned that some teachers might be asked to move to new classrooms to accommodate grade-level groupings, Mrs. McDavid proclaimed, "You CAN'T move me. I've been in the same classroom for 24 years. I have seniority!"

After weighing options about how to address this problem, Mrs. Parsons distributed a memo about appropriate use of audiovisual equipment to all teachers.

She attached a copy of the local school policy governing use of this equipment and emerging technologies to the memo and placed it in the mailboxes of all teachers before 8:00 A.M. on Monday, the day of a regularly scheduled faculty meeting. Mrs. Parsons didn't mention this issue with teachers during the faculty meeting, and none of the teachers brought it up to be discussed.

Mrs. Parsons visited the library/media center again on Thursday of the same week in order to review the sign-up form for use of audiovisual equipment. No changes were made to the form after the faculty meeting and distribution of the memo. Mrs. McDavid's name continued to be listed as requesting use of the VCR/DVD equipment and TV monitor for two hours during every afternoon three weeks prior to Christmas.

Another note in red ink was written at the bottom of the form. It read, "Someone isn't teaching; instead, they are babysitting third grade students. Parents need to complain!"

As Mrs. Booker ushered a fourth grade class from the library/media center, she approached Mrs. Parsons and asked, "What am I to do? Mrs. McDavid won't take a hint! Many teachers are complaining now, and two have threatened to call parents and suggest that they file a formal complaint with our central office supervisor."

Questions

1. Looking back on your first choice for a decision, why do you think this option was unsuccessful in resolving this instructional concern with Mrs. McDavid?

2. What additional options need to be considered at this point?

3. Should you consult with the superintendent about this concern in case parents follow through with the anonymous teacher's thoughts to involve the central office?

4. What measures related to the community's needs could be used to prevent this type of problem in the future?

5. Do you think it wise to address the comments written in red ink on the sign-up form for use of audiovisual equipment in the library/media center?

Activities

1. Write a draft of a memo you would give to Mrs. McDavid individually.

2. Develop notes to include in your first faculty meeting for teachers at the beginning of the next school year that you hope will alleviate this problem.

3. Role-play a conference with Mrs. McDavid to address this concern.

4. Prepare an outline for your faculty handbook that clearly explains expectations for use of audiovisual equipment to meet instructional objectives.

5. Discuss in what ways and to what degree teachers should be involved in developing instructional policies that align with the school's mission statement.

ISLLC Standards

STANDARD 3—A school administrator is an educational leader who promotes the success of all students by ensuring management of the organization, operations, and resources for a safe, efficient, and effective learning environment.

Knowledge

The administrator has knowledge and understanding of:

- Theories and models of organizations and the principles of organizational development
- Human resources management and development
- Current technologies that support management functions

Dispositions

The administrator believes in, values, and is committed to:

- Making management decisions to enhance learning and teaching
- High-quality standards, expectations, and performances
- Involving stakeholders in management processes

Performances

The administrator facilitates processes and engages in activities ensuring that:

- Operational procedures are designed and managed to maximize opportunities for successful learning
- Operational plans and procedures to achieve the vision and goals of the school are in place
- Problems are confronted and resolved in a timely manner

STANDARD 4—A school administrator is an educational leader who promotes the success of all students by collaborating with families and community members, responding to diverse community interests and needs, and mobilizing community resources.

Knowledge

The administrator has knowledge and understanding of:

- Emerging issues and trends that potentially impact the school community
- Community resources

Dispositions

The administrator believes in, values, and is committed to:

- The proposition that families have the best interests of their children in mind

Performances

The administrator facilitates processes and engages in activities ensuring that:

- Available community resources are secured to help the school solve problems and achieve goals
- Community stakeholders are treated equitably
- Opportunities for staff to develop collaborative skills are provided

REFERENCE

Smith, W., & Andrews, R. (1989). *Instructional leadership: How principals make a difference.* Alexandria, VA: Association for Supervision and Curriculum Development.

CASE 4

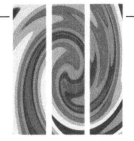

Grandmother's Medicine

A Medical Emergency at School

Metal detectors are commonplace in schools to deter students or visitors from smuggling weapons onto campus. Uniformed guards, police dogs, locker searches, and drug testing are conventional artifacts aimed at ensuring student safety. They are also measures school officials have taken to respond to societal and cultural change.

School safety means more than preventing weapons or drugs from being smuggled onto campus. Drake and Roe (2003) report that of thousands of lawsuits filed each year against schools and their employees, negligence is cited most often for injuries to students, faculty, and staff. Dangers for students involved in athletics, cheerleading, and vocational training, and even on a bus ride home after school, are subject to judicial action when someone gets hurt.

School leaders are responsible for student safety, and planning to deal with harmful situations means more than completing forms in the district's mandatory safety document. "Lockdowns" and building evacuations are examples of drills that require rehearsal so that students, faculty, and staff know exactly how to respond during a crisis, and contingency plans are essential for all emergency operations.

Safety is enhanced if school leaders implement and monitor systems that affect students. Principals must be able to identify visitors to the building, account for pupils who arrive late for school or check out early, devise efficient one-way traffic routes to handle traffic during peak times in the day, evaluate the condition of equipment and furniture on the campus and repair or replace unserviceable items promptly, inspect fire extinguishers regularly, ensure that the health clinic is fully stocked with appropriate first-aid equipment, maintain strict control over medication for students, and ensure that people who use dangerous equipment (lawn mowers, buffers, and food preparation items in the kitchen) are trained in their use. The list of potential safety risks is lengthy, and each item requires careful attention.

It is possible to anticipate and plan for many school emergencies, such as dismissing students in poor weather or safeguarding them from threats of tornados and hurricanes. One of the most difficult challenges is to maintain vigilance to ensure that the school operates safely while students and teachers devote their attention to instructional matters.

After you have developed safety plans, then what? You have met a minimum requirement by *having* them, but they are only pages in a book. Experienced school leaders know that students, teachers, and staff must *practice* emergency drills to become proficient at their duties during stressful moments. Careful analysis of the space in your building will help to make most decisions about safety procedures, but it is a best practice to consider all of the variables that affect those decisions *before* emergencies occur.

FACTORS TO CONSIDER

- Comprehensive school safety plans
- Practicing emergency drills
- Contingency plans
- Ethical behavior

THE CASE

Tom DeLancy's first semester as principal at Mountain View Elementary School was rewarding. He addressed curriculum and discipline problems that were neglected under the previous administration, and the faculty was enthusiastic about the school's steady progress under his leadership.

Mountain View is 25 miles from the central office and is the northernmost school in the district. The majority of the 1,500 people living in this isolated, tightly knit community support their families by farming or working in blue-collar jobs. Friday night high school football games always sell out despite consecutive seasons in which the team has failed to win as many games as it has lost. Each game is the topic of discussion and arguments at the community's coffee shop on Saturday morning during football season.

The school's faculty is composed of 18 regular education and two special education teachers. Two federally funded teachers and an aide are assigned to help students improve reading and mathematics scores on standardized tests.

As Tom developed safety plans for the school, one of his concerns was its isolation. A volunteer fire department was 10 miles away, but staff hours at that facility were irregular since the firemen worked at other jobs during the day. County sheriff's deputies patrolled local highways but spent most of their time in more densely populated areas.

Tom took most of the semester to get to know the faculty and community. Most parents welcomed his insistence on improved learning and attendance, but teachers continued to complain about a lack of support for homework and other academic matters.

The PTA president suggested that training the faculty and staff in CPR would be an excellent way to enhance safety and build community relations. Tom agreed and arranged for a half-day session on one of the system's professional development days before Christmas. Teachers were receptive to the idea, and only a few complained about needing the time to compile grades and attend to other classroom matters.

CPR training, provided at no cost by emergency medical technicians who worked for the largest hospital in the county, was excellent. Two teachers were absent, but the rest of the faculty enjoyed the training and the opportunity to interact with each other. Three parents took time off from work to join the session. At Tom's suggestion, Mrs. Bennett, the school secretary, noted the name of each teacher who earned CPR certification for future reference.

The Christmas holidays passed quickly and the second semester began. During the second week of classes, Tom was working in his office to complete the written portion of a teacher's evaluation when Mrs. Staley, a first grade teacher, rushed in. She carried a student in her arms.

"There's something wrong!" she said with a trembling voice. "What should I do?"

"What happened?" DeLancy asked, standing to move around the desk.

"I don't know! Steven got out of his chair to come to my desk. He took three or four steps and fainted!"

"Take him to the health clinic!"

Tom accompanied Mrs. Staley to the clinic and watched as she laid Steven on a bed.

"Now what?" she asked.

"Let's put him on the floor; it's a flat surface."

Mrs. Staley helped the principal move Steven gently to the carpet. She stood and took a step back, her body trembling.

"I don't think he's breathing," she said.

"I'm not sure if he is or not, but you go back to class. Take care of the other children."

As Mrs. Staley left the room, Mrs. Bennett appeared in the doorway.

"Is there anything I can do?"

DeLancy knew that he needed help. "Yes. Call Mrs. Roberts on the intercom. She was great during CPR training. Ask her to take her class to the library and come to the health room. Don't tell her what the problem is; there's no point in upsetting everyone."

She nodded. "Anything else?"

"Call 911. Tell them we have an emergency. Call Steven's parents, too. Tell them he fainted in class and we're trying to get him to a hospital. Ask them to come to school right away! And keep the lines clear. Take the phone off the hook when you're not making a call. We don't need to have our line tied up right now."

She returned to her office. DeLancy began to administer CPR to Steven, who was unresponsive. Within minutes Mrs. Roberts joined Tom in the clinic.

"Can I help?"

"Yes! Steven's a first grader in Mrs. Staley's room. He fainted in class and I've been giving him CPR for about three minutes," DeLancy replied, glancing at his watch."

"Mrs. Bennett is calling 911 and trying to reach Steven's parents."

Mrs. Roberts nodded and settled onto the floor next to Steven, ready to begin chest compressions.

"I'll take over here," she said. "Why don't you check on 911?"

Teachers were bringing their classes to the cafeteria for lunch. Curious about the commotion, several left their students unattended and strolled toward the health room.

One of the school's custodians appeared, and DeLancy directed him to bring three portable chalkboards to serve as a barrier between the cafeteria and health room. Mrs. Bennett told DeLancy that the hospital was dispatching a rescue helicopter, but she had been unable to reach Steven's parents. He sent her to find Mr. Sanders, a third grade teacher, to ask him to wait outside the building to guide rescuers to the school as soon as the helicopter landed.

DeLancy returned to the health room to find Mrs. Roberts continuing to administer CPR to Steven. He helped with chest compressions and breathing, but there was no change in Steven's condition.

Ten minutes later the sound of a helicopter's main rotor announced the medical team's arrival. Two paramedics rushed into the building, evaluated Steven, placed him on a gurney, and rushed him to the waiting aircraft. They promised to call DeLancy as soon as they reached the hospital and a physician examined Steven.

Mrs. Bennett told DeLancy that she had found Steven's parents and they were on their way to school. They arrived in time to board the helicopter with their son.

As soon as the aircraft left, Tom called the superintendent's office to tell him about the morning's events. The superintendent asked to be kept informed as the situation developed.

DeLancy received a call an hour later from the emergency medical technician who had promised to contact him. Steven died on the way to the hospital.

"How could that happen? What went wrong?" DeLancy asked, incredulous.

"His parents told us that Steven took some of his grandmother's heart medication during the holidays. He had his stomach pumped in the emergency room and the nurse who inserted an air tube into his throat used one that was too big. The tube cut his throat and scar tissue from the cut formed around the top of his airway. Today was the day that the tissue sealed the opening. There was nothing any of us could do. I'm sorry."

Questions

1. What should Mr. DeLancy tell the faculty about Steven's death?

2. What can the principal do to help Mrs. Staley's students cope with the loss of a classmate?

3. Where are the most dangerous places on your campus for students? What steps have been taken to reduce safety risks?

Activities

1. The superintendent asks for a written summary of the events surrounding Steven's death. He intends to give the summary to board of education members. Write a memorandum that satisfies his request.

2. What will Mr. DeLancy tell Steven's parents?

3. As Mr. DeLancy reflects on Steven's death, what safety lessons do you think he should learn?

4. How do you plan for student safety at your school? What elements of the process should be changed? Why?

ISLLC Standards

STANDARD 3–A school administrator is an educational leader who promotes the success of all students by ensuring management of the organization, operations, and resources for a safe, efficient, and effective learning environment.

Knowledge

The administrator has knowledge and understanding of:

- Principles and issues relating to school safety and security
- Legal issues impacting school operations

Dispositions

The administrator believes in, values, and is committed to:

- Accepting responsibility
- A safe environment

Performances

The administrator facilitates processes and engages in activities ensuring that:

- The school plant, equipment, and support systems operate safely, efficiently, and effectively
- Effective communication skills are used

REFERENCE

Drake, T. L., & Roe, W. H. (2003). *The principalship* (6th ed.). Upper Saddle River, NJ: Merrill Prentice Hall.

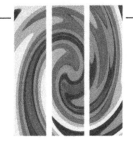

Is Dismissal Justified?

An Effective Teacher
Faces a Moral Issue

BACKGROUND

Any teenager will tell you that the rights to privacy in one's home and with personal activities are rights inherent in the words of the Fourth Amendment to the U.S. Constitution. Since the beginning of our country, citizens have enjoyed basic fundamental rights guaranteed by the Constitution such as the right to worship, the right to speak about public matters, and the right to choose a vocation of interest without fear of reprisal. So, where do limits regarding the right to privacy begin and end for educators? May male teachers be required to wear neckties or to shave facial hair at the request of the local school board? May teachers openly participate in an alternative lifestyle? Does the grade level at which they are assigned to teach make a difference in behaviors that will be considered acceptable? Responses to these questions and many others have resulted in legal challenges answered by the courts in recent times.

Courts have held teachers to a higher standard of behavior than the general population. In fact, the decision of the court in *Board of Education v. Wood* (1986) upheld the dismissal of two male teachers for smoking and providing marijuana to two 15-year-old girls at the apartment of the teachers. Despite the off-campus setting of this incident, the Supreme Court of Kentucky upheld dismissal of the teachers. The court reasoned that "a teacher is held to a standard of personal conduct which does not permit the commission of immoral or criminal acts because of the harmful impression made on the students" (*Board of Education v. Wood*, 1986).

Later, however, an Ohio court ruled:

> Allowing dismissal merely upon a showing of immoral behavior without consideration of the nexus between the conduct and fitness to teach should be an unwarranted intrusion on a teacher's right to privacy. [The] . . . court found that school officials had not produced evidence to show that an adulterous affair with another school employee constituted immorality when it did not have a hostile impact on the school community. (Cambron-McCabe, McCarthy, & Thomas, 2004, p. 415)

Other cases that have been controversial involve teachers with alternative lifestyles. In 1977, the Supreme Court of Washington upheld dismissal of a male teacher, James Gaylord, who admitted that he was homosexual when questioned by the school vice principal. The court's reasoning was that

> after Gaylord's homosexual status became publicly known, it would and did impair his teaching efficiency. A teacher's efficiency is determined by his relationship with his students, their parents, the school administration and fellow teachers. If Gaylord had not been discharged after he became known as a homosexual, the result would be fear, confusion, suspicion, parental concern and pressure on the administration by students, parents, and other teachers. (Alexander & Alexander, 2005, p. 704)

A guidance counselor employed with Mad River Local School District in Montgomery County, Ohio, was dismissed when she informed school personnel of her bisexuality and the homosexuality of two student advisees. The United States Court of Appeals for the Sixth Circuit upheld the guidance counselor's dismissal (*Rowland v. Mad River Local School District,* 1984).

Conversely, a Utah Federal District Court "ruled that the community's negative response to a teacher's homosexuality was not sufficient justification to remove the teacher as the girl's volleyball coach and instruct her not to mention her sexual orientation to students, parents, or staff" (Cambron-McCabe et al., p. 343).

Courts consider the following factors to assess a teacher's fitness to teach when immorality is an issue:

1. The age and maturity of the teacher's students

2. The likelihood that the teacher's conduct will have an adverse effect on students or other teachers

3. The degree of anticipated adversity

4. The proximity of the conduct

5. The extenuating or aggravating circumstances surrounding the conduct

6. The likelihood that the conduct would be repeated

7. The underlying motives

8. The chilling effect on the rights of teachers

SOURCE: In Re: Donna Thomas, Board of Education of Cape Girardeau School District No. 63, v. Donna Thomas, 1996.

Important to the effectiveness of school leaders is a clear understanding of the parameters and knowledge of the most recent judicial decisions related to the rights of teachers. School leaders at both the local school and central office levels are called upon to balance the rights of teachers with the needs of a school district to maintain an environment that supports the mores of the community served by the school district. When controversial situations develop, school administrators must employ skills in human resources and conflict resolution. This case requires a school administrator to balance the privacy rights of a teacher against the school's interest in maintaining a productive learning environment.

FACTORS TO CONSIDER

- Limits of teachers' right to privacy
- Constitutional rights of association
- Perceptions of teachers' standings in the community
- Employment policies that govern teacher reprimand and dismissal

THE CASE

Dr. Sam Green is known as the kind of principal who has his thumb on the pulse of George Washington High School. He has been principal of this historic high school of 1,800 students for eight years. He has enlisted help from city and community members to revitalize the school and residential area surrounding it. Four years ago, Dr. Green successfully pursued and established an International Baccalaureate (IB) Diploma Program program at George Washington High School.

Sponsored by the International Baccalaureate Organization, the IB program requires students aged 16 to 19 to participate in rigorous preuniversity courses and examinations that meet the needs of highly motivated secondary school students. This program is designed as a comprehensive two-year curriculum that allows its graduates to fulfill requirements of various national education systems. The diploma model is based on the pattern of no single country but incorporates the best elements of several and is available in English, French, and Spanish (International Baccalaureate Program, 2006).

Because George Washington is the first and only high school to offer an IB program, student enrollment has increased from 1,200 to 1,350 students from population growth in the attendance zone served by the school and from approved transfer requests from students seeking to participate in the IB program.

Despite the size of the high school and the large number of faculty members, Dr. Green prides himself on his knowledge of all faculty members. He makes a point to learn the names of employees' family members and to learn about hobbies or special interests pursued by faculty members.

One of George Washington's most revered teachers is Mr. Mark Downs, who teaches senior AP English and an elective course in British literature. Before beginning his teaching career, Mr. Downs served four years in the United States Marine Corps. He served his country in Desert Storm and was awarded a medal for bravery in combat.

A veteran teacher of 15 years, Mr. Downs has served as faculty sponsor of the debate team for 11 years. He fully supported Dr. Green's plans to establish an IB program and was the first teacher to request an appointment to the IB faculty. Although he has never married, other faculty members have described Mr. Downs and the woman he dates as a permanent item. In fact, fellow faculty members in the English Department routinely tease Mr. Downs about hearing wedding bells in the near future.

During October of this school year, Mr. Downs submitted a request for a personal day on a Friday, which Dr. Green readily approved. Mr. Downs didn't specify a reason for the request as board policy does not require an explanation. Dr. Green did not give another thought to the circumstance of Mr. Downs's personal leave day, until he approached the George Washington front drive and parking lot on the following Monday morning. The first thing that Dr. Green noticed as he parked his car was a sign positioned in the center of the front lawn of the school. The sign read, "Beware, Mr. Downs has a boyfriend. You know what that means!"

After parking his car, Dr. Green pulled up the sign, and then he noticed other signs with similar messages taped to the entryway of the school and placed in the ground on corners of the school property. Dr. Green asked the head custodian to survey the school building and property to remove additional signs that might be displayed. Dr. Green was confused about this Monday morning greeting, but he knew he had a problem to investigate and address. He e-mailed Mr. Downs, requesting a conference during Mr. Downs's planning time beginning at 10:30 A.M.

As it turned out, the conference with Mr. Downs wasn't scheduled soon enough. Dr. Green received reports as early as 8:45 A.M. that students in Mr. Downs's class were loud and disruptive. During both second and third periods, three to four students in each of Mr. Downs's early classes heckled him. They made references to seeing Mr. Downs in a TV news telecast filmed in the nearby city of San Alito and aired Saturday evening at 6 P.M. During the weekend, the city of San Alito allowed a parade celebrating Gay Pride Week. When participants in the parade were interviewed by a local news commentator, Mr. Downs was filmed standing on the sidewalk holding hands with another man. Of the footage taped covering the Gay Pride parade, this particular segment was chosen to be aired on national networks. Not only was it included in newscasts at 6 P.M. that Saturday evening; it was also shown as part of the news broadcast at 10 P.M. Saturday night, and Sunday morning at 7 A.M.

When it was finally 10:30 A.M., Dr. Green saw Mr. Downs at the receptionist's counter and motioned for him to come into the principal's office. Three students, two male and one female, were sitting in office chairs. They had been referred to the office for disciplinary violations in Mr. Downs's early morning classes. These three students were the main instigators of the disruption in Mr. Downs's classes. As the assistant principal, Mr. Tones, stood reading the students' disciplinary referrals, Dr. Green asked him to postpone dealing with the students until Mr. Downs had a chance to explain the weekend's events. Dr. Green asked Mr. Tones to join the conference with Mr. Downs.

Once the two administrators and Mr. Downs were seated in the inner administrative office, Dr. Green said, "Help me out here, Mark. What in the world's going on?"

"I don't know where to begin or how to explain this situation to you, Dr. Green," answered Mark Downs. "I'm not part of the gay scene. I went to San Alito this weekend to see my college roommate, Ron, who is gay. He lives in Canada now, and despite his alternative lifestyle, we've remained friends. I just wanted to visit with him and talk about old times. Just as the camera started filming, Ron took my hand, because he wanted to point out another former college buddy who was in the parade. We weren't holding hands as a couple would. It just looked that way to the camera."

"Mark, you know how conservative this community is. I've already received calls from two local ministers and the mayor. And the superintendent called to tell me that his office has received numerous calls from parents about the news broadcast. Three students are sitting in the office for creating disruptions in your classes, and the news broadcast is the topic of conservation among all students *and* teachers. This is a tough one, Mark; I'm just not sure how to handle it."

Just as Dr. Green made this remark, the telephone on his desk rang. He picked it up to hear the excited voice of the secretary say, "Dr. Green, a news announcer from WKAT is here with a cameraman. They want to see you and to film footage in the school hallways. What should I tell them?"

Questions

1. Who should be involved in discussions about resolving this situation?

2. To what degree should Dr. Green try to support Mr. Downs?

3. How should students referred to the office for creating disruptions in Mr. Downs's classes be dealt with?

4. Should Dr. Green speak to the news announcer? If so, what should he say?

5. What should Dr. Green do to minimize disruption in Mr. Downs's afternoon classes?

Activities

1. Role-play a conference between Dr. Green and the superintendent regarding the weekend incident.

2. Write an announcement to explain Mr. Downs's predicament to teachers and students.

3. List options for resolving this situation.

4. Write a memo to the superintendent describing the situation involving Mr. Downs.

5. Write a memo to the superintendent recommending dismissal of Mr. Downs. Justify your decision.

ISLLC Standards

STANDARD 2—A school administrator is an educational leader who promotes the success of all students by advocating, nurturing, and sustaining a school culture and instructional program conducive to student learning and staff professional growth.

Knowledge

- Diversity and its meaning for educational programs
- School cultures

Dispositions

- The benefits that diversity brings to the school community
- A safe and supportive learning environment

Performances

- All individuals are treated with fairness, dignity, and respect
- The responsibilities and contributions of each individual are acknowledged
- Diversity is considered in developing learning experiences

STANDARD 3—A school administrator is an educational leader who promotes the success of all students by ensuring management of the organization, operations, and resources for a safe, efficient, and effective learning environment.

Knowledge

The administrator has knowledge and understanding of:

- Principles and issues relating to school safety and security
- Legal issues impacting school operations

Dispositions

The administrator believes in, values, and is committed to:

- Taking risks to improve schools
- A safe environment

Performances

- Stakeholders are involved in decisions affecting schools.
- Effective problem-framing and problem-solving skills are used.

REFERENCES

Alexander, K., & Alexander, D. (2005). *American public school law* (6th ed.). Belmont, CA: Wadsworth.

Board of Education v. Wood, 717 S.W.2d 837 (Ky. 1986).

Cambron-McCabe, N. H., McCarthy, M. M., & Thomas, S. B. (2004). *Public school law* (5th ed.). Boston: Pearson Education.

In Re: Donna Thomas, Board of Education of Cape Girardeau School District No. 63, v. Donna Thomas, 926 S.W.2nd 163 (Mo. ED Div. Two 1996).

International Baccalaureate Program. (2005, November 20). IB diploma program. Retrieved June 19, 2006, from http://www.ebu1.org/main/Academic program/IB/ib.html

Rowland v. Mad River Local School District, 730 F.2d 444 (6th Cir. 1984).

CASE 6

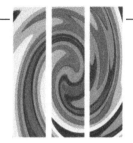

School Property Is Missing

An Employee Is Caught Stealing

A school administrator's actions and decisions are under constant scrutiny. Solving problems at school is difficult enough, but decisions made in the best interests of children sometimes have unanticipated consequences. Leaders in all organizations must learn to "live in a fishbowl" and contend with organizational politics.

School leaders must have basic competencies if they intend to become successful. As important as those competencies are, they are technical skills that may be acquired through mentoring and practice. The challenges of leadership test a principal's ethical beliefs and standards. As Gorton and Schneider (1991) remind us, "every administrator should attempt to maintain high professional ethical standards to make a more positive contribution to the improvement of education in the school" (p. 584).

The behavior of administrators is so important that a task force representing the National Association of Secondary School Principals, National Association of Elementary School Principals, American Association of School Administrators, American Association of School Personnel Administrators, and National Council of Administrative Women in Education revised their *Statement of Ethics* in 1991 to affirm that "an educational administrator's professional behavior must conform to an ethical code" that is "idealistic and at the same time practical" (Gorton and Schneider, p. 585).

An educational administrator is expected to

1. Make the well-being of students the fundamental value in all decision making and actions

2. Fulfill professional responsibilities with honesty and integrity

3. Support the principle of due process and protect the civil and human rights of all individuals

4. Obey local, state, and national laws

5. Implement the governing board of education's policies and administrative rules and regulations

6. Pursue appropriate measures to correct those laws, policies, and regulations that are not consistent with sound educational goals

7. Avoid using positions for personal gain through political, social, religious, economic, or other influence

8. Accept academic degrees or professional certification only from duly accredited institutions

9. Maintain the standards and seek to improve the effectiveness of the profession through research and continuing professional development

10. Honor all contracts until fulfillment, release, or dissolution mutually agreed on by all parties to a contract

Skills acquired in graduate course work and during clinical experiences will help prospective administrators to understand leadership's technical competencies, but subscribing to a code of ethical standards is equally important.

FACTORS TO CONSIDER

- Supervision of subordinates
- School compliance with district, state, and federal requirements
- Ethical standards and behavior
- Interpersonal relationship skills

THE CASE

Bob Tunnell's first semester as principal at Weston Elementary School went well. He visited classrooms frequently and displayed a keen interest in curriculum that his 22 teachers appreciated. The PTA supported school programs, and parents were pleased with the principal's willingness to talk with them, a courtesy his predecessor had considered a nuisance.

As Bob thought about areas in the school needing improvement, school lunches warranted consideration because they were unpopular with students. He had heard children use the term *mystery meat* on more than one occasion to describe what they had received in the serving line. He had received nearly 20 letters and phone calls from parents who complained about cafeteria workers' rudeness and the frequency with which deep-fried foods were served.

Mrs. Collinwood, the Child Nutrition Program (CNP) manager, lived in the community and had worked at Weston for almost 25 years. When Tunnell discussed parents' complaints about food quality with her, she gave them little credence. She made small concessions regarding menu items, but lunches continued to have high-fat content and low nutritional value.

Bob talked with Denise Roman, the district CNP supervisor, and learned that she had been working closely with Mrs. Collinwood to improve food quality at Weston, but without much success. The manager changed menus until complaints subsided but soon returned to using menus she preferred.

Tunnell was surprised several weeks later when Mrs. Cole, a member of the school's CNP staff, stopped by his office after she finished work. She had impressed him with her friendly, outgoing manner with children and the way in which she managed to smile during hectic times on the serving line.

"May I see you for a few minutes?" she asked. "I have a problem that I think you should know about." Her co-verbal behavior betrayed anxiety.

"Certainly. Please sit down," Tunnell replied, motioning her to a chair. He stood and walked around his desk to sit close to Mrs. Cole. "What problem do you think I should know about?"

"Well," she began, "it's Mrs. Collinwood. I think she's stealing milk from the cafeteria every day."

Bob was surprised. "Why do you think she's stealing milk?"

"Because she leaves here every day with at least two crates full of milk the children didn't drink with their lunch," she replied.

Further discussion revealed that Mrs. Collinwood had instructed her staff to remove unopened milk cartons from students' trays when they were returned for washing. The half-pint cartons were stored in a refrigerator until the CNP staff left for the day. The manager loaded the cartons into the trunk of her car before leaving campus and had been taking unopened milk home for several years.

"Please don't tell Mrs. Collinwood that I told you about the milk," Mrs. Cole said, tears streaming from her eyes. "She'll give me the worst jobs in the kitchen every day to force me to quit."

Mr. Tunnell assured Mrs. Cole that he would not betray her confidence and waited until she left before calling Mrs. Roman to relate what Mrs. Cole had said. He learned that federal food service regulations specify that unopened milk must be discarded; it cannot be used after being served.

Since Tunnell had promised Mrs. Cole that he would not reveal her as the information source, he would have to prove Mrs. Collinwood was stealing milk before taking corrective action. He asked one of the school's custodians to cut the lawn the next day near the cafeteria's loading dock at the time the manager usually left and to tell him if Mrs. Collinwood put anything into her car.

After being informed that she had placed two large containers of milk cartons inside her car's trunk, Tunnell called the central office immediately, only to discover that the superintendent was attending a conference out of town. He phoned Mrs. Roman, who told him that she would handle the matter. Bob left for the day believing that he had behaved ethically, although regretting the hardship Mrs. Collinwood would undoubtedly experience.

He arrived at school early the next morning and found Mrs. Collinwood waiting for him, so he invited her into his office.

"I wish you had talked to me about the milk before you called the superintendent and Mrs. Roman," she began.

"Why? You knew you weren't supposed to take milk home with you."

"I wasn't stealing, but now I've been suspended until the board of education holds a hearing," she said, tears welling in her eyes.

"I'm sorry, Mrs. Collinwood, but I was told that you've been taking milk for quite some time. It's my job to investigate reports like that. I'm curious, though. What could you possibly do with that much milk every day?"

She returned his gaze through moist eyes. "These kids won't drink low-fat milk and that's all I took. I gave it to my husband's hunting dogs. I hated to throw it out!"

Questions

1. Were Mr. Tunnell's actions and decisions ethical? Why or why not?

2. What would you have done with the information Mrs. Cole brought to you?

3. As a school administrator, what responsibilities do you have for the school breakfast and lunch programs?

4. What do you think should happen to Mrs. Collinwood? Why?

5. What will you say to parents who ask about the incident? Should you tell your faculty about it?

Activities

1. The superintendent decided that Mrs. Collinwood should receive a written reprimand and asks you to draft that document for his review. Write the letter. What elements must you include?

2. Role-play the conference between Mr. Tunnell and Mrs. Collinwood. What point of view do you think each participant has at the outset of the meeting?

3. Make a list of ethical values you believe a school administrator must have as an effective leader. Compare your list with the lists of others in your class. Which values appear most frequently?

ISLLC Standards

STANDARD 5—A school administrator is an educational leader who promotes the success of all students by acting with integrity, fairness, and in an ethical manner.

Knowledge

The administrator has knowledge and understanding of:

- Various ethical frameworks and perspectives on ethics
- Professional codes of ethics

Dispositions

The administrator believes in, values, and is committed to:

- Bringing ethical principles to the decision-making process
- Subordinating one's own interest to the good of the school and community

Performances

The administrator:

- Demonstrates values, beliefs, and attitudes that inspire others to higher levels of performance
- Considers the impact of one's administrative practice on others

REFERENCE

Gorton, R., & Schneider, G. (1991). *School-based leadership: Challenges and opportunities* (3rd ed.). New York: McGraw-Hill.

CASE 7

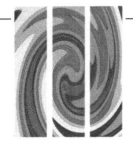

Who Has the Missing Crayons?

Dealing With Chronic Theft

Students come from many different and varied backgrounds. Some students are fortunate to be raised by parents with the economic means to give them everything they need and most of what they want. Other students grow up in households with adequate resources that need to be budgeted and conserved for special needs and opportunities. And there are students born to very limited economic means or poverty; these are the students who come to school without needed materials and instructional supplies. They often wear hand-me-down clothes and are approved as eligible for the United States Department of Agriculture (USDA) free and reduced-price lunch program.

When teachers and principals work in schools that serve students of different economic backgrounds, they must employ measures to minimize the differences and to support students living in homes of limited economic means. Their efforts need to be accomplished in subtle ways so that attention is not focused on the economic means of students. One difficulty that sometimes develops when economic disparity is evident among students in a classroom or school is theft.

The incidence of theft can be difficult to resolve while authority figures are trying to instill appropriate values of honesty and trustworthiness in students. When money or a student's jacket or the like is missing, school officials must be careful to follow school board and local school policy. It is important from professional and legal perspectives that students under suspicion of a serious school offense such as theft be guaranteed the right of protection against an unconstitutional search.

Elementary school students have fewer places to hide stolen objects; the only places readily available to them are their clothing, their desk, or a book bag. Middle school students typically have access to lockers and can use them to hide stolen objects. In addition to these hiding places, high school students also may have access to a car parked on the school campus.

If school officials decide that searching a student's clothing, purse or book bag, locker, or car is warranted, they must be careful to observe the student's constitutional right to be protected against unreasonable search and seizure guaranteed by the Fourth Amendment to the U.S. Constitution. The basic tenets of due process protected by the Fifth and Fourteenth amendments require school officials to offer students notice, and a fair and impartial hearing. Notice can be extended by explaining why the student was referred to the office. A hearing can be accomplished by simply asking the student to tell his or her side of the disciplinary incident. To offer a student a fair and impartial hearing, a school official needs to maintain a calm demeanor and listen carefully to the student's description of the incident without displaying a predetermined judgment about current or past incidents. In fact, wise administrators will take time to gather as much information as possible about an incident from all available witnesses before assigning consequences. Depending on the seriousness of the incident and the value of the stolen object, school officials may need to involve the school counselor or school psychologist or the student's parent(s).

Before beginning a search, school officials need to determine that they have reasonable suspicion to conduct the search. A school official must be prepared to address questions related to what was stolen and when a student could have had the opportunity to steal the object. School officials need to be able to justify the search based on reasonable suspicion of behavior that was directly observed, reported by witnesses, or supported by facts.

Once reasonable suspicion is reached, school officials should be careful to conduct a search in a reasonable manner. While courts have supported the authority of school officials to search students' purses, book bags, and lockers upon reasonable suspicion, school officials must be careful to conduct the search in a reasonable manner (*New Jersey v. TLO* [1985]). Unless deemed absolutely necessary, school officials should not conduct a strip search of a student. In those rare cases when a strip search is necessary, school officials are wise to have a professional witness of the same gender as the student present.

Because of recent incidents of violence in schools, some high schools have begun to use metal detectors as students enter the school building. School officials' responsibility to provide a safe, secure school environment outweighs the minimal intrusion on student rights caused by the metal detector. There are occasions when school officials feel it necessary to use dogs to conduct a drug-detecting search of school areas. Again, it is prudent for school officials to be able to justify individualized suspicion when using drug-detecting dogs. Although some lower courts (*Commonwealth v. Cass* [1998]) have reasoned that using canines does not constitute a search, other lower courts have reasoned that the use of canines does indeed constitute a search (*Kuehn v. Reston School District No. 403* [1985]).

When police officers are involved in searching a student or a student's property at school, a higher standard regarding the legality of the search is invoked. When police officers are involved, probable cause is required for the search to proceed. Probable cause requires that those conducting the search be able to support the search with specific facts related to an incident; this is a higher standard than reasonable suspicion, which requires that the person conducting the search give evidence that the search is necessary.

When confronted with an incident of theft, school officials must weigh different options and determine that reasonable suspicion is justified to conduct a search. Moreover, school officials need to consider the age of students involved, the value of the object that is missing, and types of evidence or facts that support their suspicions. Students under suspicion of theft must be afforded due process rights of notice, and a fair and impartial hearing. Finally, school officials have to make a judgment about if and when to place a call to parents or to seek help from law enforcement officers.

FACTORS TO CONSIDER

- Different approaches to disciplinary incidents of theft
- Moral and principled dimensions of student discipline
- Ethical decision making
- Communication of district and school policies and school procedures
- Socioeconomic tensions in schools

THE CASE

Serving as principal of Fairmont Elementary School for the past eight years has been a challenging and rewarding position for Mrs. Marcie Simmons. Many changes have taken place in the school community since she was first appointed principal. Then the student population at the school numbered approximately 415; currently, the total stands at just under 750 students.

Much of this population growth is due to an influx of minority students of Hispanic background. An industrial park located on the south side of the campus has experienced strong economic growth and has provided jobs for people with maintenance and hourly wage employment skills. Eight years ago, a nearby public housing project was sparsely populated. Today, the housing project has a waiting list of families seeking low-income housing.

In addition to the housing project, Fairmont Elementary School serves students whose parents live in moderate to upscale subdivisions on the north side of its attendance zone. The occupations of these parents range from supervisory factory positions to professions such as law and medicine. Approximately 30 percent of the parents are employed by a large medical center as technicians, nurses, doctors, and business office managers.

This increasing disparity in the socioeconomic levels of students in the community is a problem that teachers and Mrs. Simmons have recognized and made plans to address. When the faculty and staff reviewed their school improvement goals as part of regional accreditation last fall, teachers identified the following goal: *Implement strategies to increase students' understanding and appreciation of people from different socioeconomic backgrounds.*

School board policy requires Mrs. Simmons to distribute a *Student Code of Conduct* at the beginning of every school year. Parents are asked to sign a statement acknowledging receipt of the pamphlet. Theft of school materials or belongings of other students is a Class 2 offense. Penalties for theft range from on-campus suspension for three days to off-campus suspension for eight days. The consequences for individual students depend on the value of the objects stolen and the number of previous offenses committed by the student.

At 10:30 A.M. this morning, Miss Greenhorn submitted a disciplinary incident report to Mrs. Simmons. Miss Greenhorn suspects that Ginny, one of her fourth grade students, is responsible for stealing a box of brand-new crayons from another fourth grade student, Matt. Matt's dad is a laboratory technician at the local medical center and is able to provide school supplies for his son. In fact, Miss Greenhorn noted that some students are envious that Matt always has the newest and best clothes and school supplies.

Even though Miss Greenhorn is a second-year teacher, she has demonstrated an ability to handle classroom management effectively. The only disciplinary incidents she has reported to the office have been of a serious nature and after she has exhausted all possible classroom measures.

Mrs. Simmons logged on to the student disciplinary incident screen and searched for Ginny's name. She recalled other incidents of theft attributed to Ginny. In fact, Ginny's disciplinary record includes six prior incidents during this school year and nine incidents from the previous year when she was in third grade. During this school year, Ginny admitted to stealing another student's granola snack on two occasions. She also admitted to stealing another student's sweater because, she said, "It was a pretty color" that she liked. The other three incidents recorded for this year involved school supplies and were resolved when the objects were anonymously returned. When she was in third grade, Ginny admitted to stealing $2 from a student so that she could pay for a ticket to a play presented by a traveling troupe at school. She also admitted to stealing a pair of scissors from her teacher because, Ginny explained, she left hers at home and needed scissors for an art activity. The other six incidents noted during Ginny's third grade year were resolved when the objects were anonymously returned. Conferences with Ginny's mom were held following each of the incidents to which Ginny confessed.

As Mrs. Simmons scrolled down the screen, she read a note entered by Miss Greenhorn last month. It recounted the teacher's efforts to help Ginny understand the consequences of theft as she grows older. Miss Greenhorn documented two conferences with Ginny's mom, who is a single parent with two other younger children. Ginny's mom works the night shift at an area hotel, leaving Ginny to babysit the other children while she is at work. Also entered in Ginny's disciplinary record were dates when the school counselor met with her. Upon Miss Greenhorn's referral a month ago, the school counselor, Mrs. Davis, met with Ginny on a weekly basis. Despite this intervention, Ginny has again been referred to the office under suspicion of committing theft.

It was now 11:00 A.M. Mrs. Simmons looked away from her computer screen to see Miss Greenhorn standing in her office doorway. Mrs. Simmons motioned for Miss Greenhorn to come in and sit down in the chair across from her desk. As Mrs. Simmons shook her head in dismay, Miss Greenhorn asked, "What are we going to do? I haven't announced to the class that a brand new box of crayons has been stolen from Matt as yet. If I do, Ginny will just return the crayons anonymously, which won't really help her. When I've contacted Ginny's mom in the past, her mom defends Ginny's denial of stealing. The counselor scheduled regular sessions each week during this last month to counsel with Ginny. What steps can we take to help Ginny understand how serious stealing is?"

Questions

Assume you are the principal as you respond to these questions:

1. What is your initial response to Miss Greenhorn?

2. What is your first course of action regarding this incident?

3. Identify the school district and local school policies that pertain to this incident.

4. How can you involve the parent in a way that will help you resolve this incident appropriately?

5. What techniques should be implemented in the classroom to reduce attention to the disparities in the socioeconomic status of students and to increase student acceptance of people of different socioeconomic backgrounds?

Activities

1. Role-play a conference with Miss Greenhorn about this newest incidence of theft.

2. Discuss the various options available to resolve this incident and serve Ginny's best interests for the future.

3. Identify resources outside the school district that could be available to help Ginny.

4. Outline points to address with Ginny's mother in a formal conference.

5. Draft a memo to your counselor requesting additional help for Ginny.

ISLLC Standards

STANDARD 3—A school administrator is an educational leader who promotes the success of all students by ensuring management of the organization, operations, and resources for a safe, efficient, and effective learning environment.

Knowledge

The administrator has knowledge and understanding of:
- Operational procedures at the school and district level
- Principles and issues relating to school safety and security
- Legal issues impacting school operations

Dispositions

- Making management decisions to enhance learning and teaching
- High-quality standards, expectations, and performances
- A safe environment

Performances

- Potential problems and opportunities are identified.
- Problems are confronted and resolved in a timely manner.
- A safe, clean, and aesthetically pleasing school environment is created and maintained.

STANDARD 4—A school administrator is an educational leader who promotes the success of all students by collaborating with families and community members, responding to diverse community interests and needs, and mobilizing community resources.

Knowledge

- Community resources

Dispositions

- Collaboration and communication with families
- Resources of the family and community needing to be brought to bear on the education of students

Performances

- There is outreach to different business, religious, political, and service agencies and organizations.
- Available community resources are secured to help the school solve problems and achieve goals.
- Community youth family services are integrated with school programs.

STANDARD 5—A school administrator is an educational leader who promotes the success of all students by acting with integrity, fairness, and in an ethical manner.

Knowledge

- Various ethical frameworks and perspectives on ethics

Dispositions

- Bringing ethical principles to the decision-making process
- Using the influence of one's office constructively and productively in the service of all students and their families

Performances

- ■ Treats people fairly, equitably, and with dignity and respect
- ■ Applies laws and procedures fairly, wisely, and considerately

REFERENCES

Commonwealth v. Cass, 709 A.2d 350 (Pa. 1998).
Kuehn v. Reston School District No. 403, 103 Wash. 2d 594, 694 P.2d 1078 (1985).
New Jersey v. T.L.O., 469 U.S. 325, 342 n. 8 (1985).

CASE 8

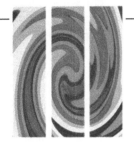

A Good Student Earns Detention

Poor Grades for Misbehavior at School

America has been deeply involved in transforming schools for the last 25 years. Owens (1995) wrote that the first wave of reform began in 1983 with the publication of *A Nation at Risk,* which produced "an astonishing increase in regulatory mandates imposed on the schools by the states" (p. 96). The regulations were designed to accomplish what the public had been persuaded to believe the schools were incapable of doing: specifying textbooks to be used, mandating how many minutes should be devoted to instruction, identifying the most effective teaching techniques, and creating comprehensive systems of testing and reporting that could be monitored by governmental agencies.

The 1990s ushered in a second wave of change. Reform during this decade was based on a belief that individual schools were able to recognize and remedy their own deficiencies. Thus, it was believed that teachers involved in action research in their classrooms could correct most problems associated with teaching and learning. And school leaders could promote improvement by empowering their faculties to change organizational procedures that were detrimental to learning and to give them sufficient autonomy to transform schools.

The 1990s collaborative model has given way to a structured, data-driven method inherent in regulatory compliance with provisions of the No Child Left Behind Act (NCLB). Since its approval in 2002, states and school districts have struggled to hire and retain Highly Qualified teachers, locate adequate numbers of special educators, close performance gaps between children of different socioeconomic and ethnic groups, and attain Adequate Yearly Progress, an externally imposed measure of success created to hold schools accountable for their students' academic achievements.

NCLB is another effort to reform America's schools. Its provisions challenge principals and teachers to balance professional and personal beliefs about school and children to meet its requirements. The stresses associated with having all students, regardless of ability, attain predetermined levels of achievement may take their toll on learning. As Siepert and Likert (1973) reported, "The main causes of organizational effectiveness or ineffectiveness are the organizational climate and the leadership behavior which significantly affect how subordinates deal with each other individually and in work groups in order to produce the end results" (p. 3).

FACTORS TO CONSIDER

- Organizational effectiveness
- Systemic problems in schools
- Communication skills
- Classroom management
- Differences between academic and behavioral standards

THE CASE

Orchard Street Elementary School is seven years old and was built to alleviate overcrowded conditions in two other schools in the southern part of the district. The building was designed to accommodate 600 students and had four unoccupied classrooms when it opened.

Mrs. Cindy Grable was selected as Orchard Street's first principal from among nine applicants. She had been a teacher for six years and an assistant principal and principal for four more. Although the challenges of opening a new school were daunting, Cindy was enthusiastic about hiring a quality staff and helping children to learn. She had been successful in other leadership positions but wanted a chance to do things *her* way.

Cindy and her faculty, which consisted of two teachers in each grade, kindergarten through six, and a special education teacher and an aide, went through "growing pains" as they worked to meet the needs of their new community. The faculty spent many hours discussing curriculum improvements and teaching strategies. As student achievement and community support increased, Orchard Street's reputation as a "good" school spread.

New housing developments soon encircled the school; enrollment increased by 50 percent in four years. Teachers were added to the faculty, but the number of students in each class continued to grow. Cindy was disappointed when the board of education assigned four portable classrooms to the campus in response to parents' complaints about crowded conditions, but she saw no alternative to the board's decision.

Space became a constraint. The cafeteria, which also served as an auditorium, was too small to seat everyone for assemblies. Events were presented first to the primary grades in one meeting and then to the elementary children in another.

Lunchtime was hectic. Children had difficulty moving through the serving lines, taking trays to tables, and having enough time to eat. Parents and teachers complained about the split-second timing lunch required.

Cindy and her teachers knew there was little they could do about overcrowding. They tried to maintain a positive attitude, but the telltale signs of stress were beginning to show.

Despite crowded conditions, Orchard Street Elementary made Adequate Yearly Progress on standardized tests, but Cindy wondered how long that would last. Nearly all of the school's classrooms had more students assigned than state rules permitted.

As the year progressed, Cindy noticed an increase in student misbehavior and wondered if the school's assertive discipline plan needed to be revised. More students than usual were assigned to detention halls and in-school suspensions. At first she attributed the change to a larger enrollment. The faculty discussed its disciplinary procedures several times but was committed to enforcing the few general rules for student conduct that had served Orchard Street so well in past years.

Three weeks after spring break, Cindy visited the extended day program offered in the cafeteria each day after school to help parents who worked and didn't want their children at home for several hours without supervision. As she talked with students about classes, homework, and other topics, Cindy was approached by Don and Laura Newcomb, the parents of two students in the school and active PTA members. Laura had worked as an aide for several years.

Cindy smiled and extended her hand in greeting.

"Well, hello," she said warmly. "I didn't know your girls were in the extended day program."

The parents exchanged glances. Both wore worried expressions.

"They're not, Mrs. Grable," Don replied after looking at his wife for reassurance.

Sensing their discomfort, Cindy asked them to follow her to the office.

"What seems to be the problem?" She asked after Don and Laura were seated.

"Mrs. Grable, you know we're not complaining parents. We support the PTA and the teachers. We're very proud of our school," Laura said.

Cindy smiled. "I am, too, and much of the success we've had is due to parents like you and Don and the way you've raised your children."

Laura returned Cindy's smile. "Well, we have a problem and we need your help."

Cindy leaned forward. "Tell me what I can do."

Don cleared his throat before speaking. "Tonya came home today with a note from Mrs. Fitzsimmons that she'd have detention hall next Tuesday."

Cindy was surprised. Tonya was a fourth-grade honor-roll student and a member of the student council, and she had been chosen as "Student of the Week" recently. As far as the principal could recall, Tonya had never been in trouble at school.

"Did Mrs. Fitzsimmons explain why Tonya would be in detention hall?"

Cindy had learned from experience that some teachers were better than others at record keeping, but she had explained to the faculty that parents had a right to know the infractions their children had committed if they were punished with either detention hall or in-school suspension.

"No," Laura replied, "and Tonya doesn't know either."

Cindy was surprised. All of her teachers used an assertive discipline program that meant recording a student's name on the class chalkboard for the first offense of the day and check marks for subsequent problems. Children were assigned to detention hall only after their name and four check marks in one day appeared on the board.

"I'm disappointed that Mrs. Fitzsimmons couldn't tell you how Tonya earned detention hall. Have you talked with her?"

"We called her last night," Don replied. "Tonya interrupted a reading lesson once and grabbed a ball during physical education from someone when she shouldn't have. We understand her having a name and a check on the board, but Mrs. Fitzsimmons gave her three more checks for not completing her math homework."

"Are you sure Tonya was punished for not doing homework?" Cindy asked.

"That's what Mrs. Fitzsimmons said," Laura replied. "We don't think that's fair. Isn't the assertive discipline program designed to handle behavior problems?"

"Yes," the principal nodded, "it is." After a moment's thought, she added, "Let me talk to Mrs. Fitzsimmons to understand her reasons for assigning a detention hall, and I'll call you to let you know what I've learned."

Both parents stood and thanked Cindy. They assured her that they weren't looking for favors for their children, but wanted to understand the school's rules.

As soon as the Newcombs left, Cindy walked through the darkened halls toward the fourth grade classrooms. She was reassured to see light coming from Mrs. Fitzsimmons's classroom. The teacher was working on a bulletin board when the principal entered. Cindy noticed the names of more than one-half the students in the class listed on the board. Most had two or three check marks.

"Hi, Marie."

"Oh, hello, Cindy," the teacher replied, students' spelling tests in one hand, a stapler in the other. "What brings you to the fourth grade this late in the day?"

"Can we sit and talk for a moment? If this isn't a good time . . ."

"Oh, no," Mrs. Fitzsimmons said, "this is fine. I'm almost finished, anyway." She motioned for Cindy to join her at a table at the back of the room.

"I just had a conference with the Newcombs," the principal began. "They're concerned about Tonya being assigned to detention hall."

"Well, they should be," Mrs. Fitzsimmons replied. "Her work habits have really slipped since midyear!"

"Are you having trouble with the children?" Cindy asked. "I noticed that you have quite a few names and checks on the board," she said, gesturing toward the front of the classroom.

"Yes, I am. We all are. In fact, the fourth grade team met before spring break and decided to get tough with the kids. Every year at this time they forget about school when baseball and softball tryouts begin. They stay up late for games and don't have time for homework; they come to school too tired to learn. They're so irresponsible, and their parents let them get away with it!" Mrs. Fitzsimmons's voice was filled with frustration.

"Is that what happened to Tonya? She missed turning in an assignment?"

"Yes, she did. She didn't even try to complete her math homework last Tuesday, so she earned three checks along with a name and a check for other misbehavior."

The principal paused for a moment. "And the other fourth grade teachers are giving checks for incomplete assignments, too?" she asked.

"Yes, we are. We have to teach the children that work comes before play," Mrs. Fitzsimmons replied.

"I'd like to meet with the team to discuss this," Cindy said as she stood to leave.

"All right, but I hope you're not thinking of changing what we're doing. I know the other teachers feel the same as I do. We've got to get these children to be more responsible!"

"Let's talk about it tomorrow after school," Cindy said as she walked toward the door.

Questions

What will Cindy say to the fourth grade teachers at the meeting? What issues should she discuss?

1. What will Cindy tell the Newcombs? Will Tonya have to report to detention hall?

2. Based on your professional experience, are certain times during the school year more hectic than others?

3. How can a principal alleviate some of the stress associated with the most difficult periods?

4. Does anyone else need to know about this incident?

Activities

1. Role-play the conference between Mrs. Grable, Mrs. Fitzsimmons, and the other two fourth grade teachers.

2. Write a memorandum to your faculty to remind them about the appropriate use of the school's assertive discipline program.

3. Do you think the fourth grade teachers might feel that Mrs. Grable is not supporting their decision?

4. If Mr. and Mrs. Newcomb hadn't approached Mrs. Grable with Tonya's problem, in what ways might she have discovered the reason for an increased number of students being assigned to detention hall?

ISLLC Standards

STANDARD 2—A school administrator is an educational leader who promotes the success of all students by advocating, nurturing, and sustaining a school culture and instructional program conducive to student learning and staff professional growth.

Knowledge

The administrator has knowledge and understanding of:

- Student growth and development
- Applied learning theories

Dispositions

The administrator believes in, values, and is committed to:

- Student learning as the fundamental purpose of schooling
- A safe and supportive learning environment

Performances

The administrator facilitates processes and engages in activities ensuring that:

- All individuals are treated with fairness, dignity, and respect
- The school is organized and aligned for success

STANDARD 5—A school administrator is an educational leader who promotes the success of all students by acting with integrity, fairness, and in an ethical manner.

Knowledge

The administrator has knowledge and understanding of:

- Various ethical frameworks and perspectives on ethics
- Professional code of ethics

Dispositions

The administrator believes in, values, and is committed to:

- Bringing ethical principles to the decision-making process
- Development of a caring school community

Performances

The administrator:

- Demonstrates a personal and professional code of ethics
- Considers the impact of one's administrative practices on others

REFERENCES

Owens, R. F. (1998). *Organizational behavior in education* (6th ed.). Boston: Allyn & Bacon.

Siepert, A. F., & Likert, R. (1973). *The Likert school profile measurements of the human organization.* Paper presented to the American Educational Research Association National Convention, February 27, 1973.

CASE 9

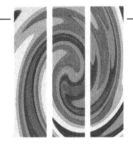

Copyright and the Computer

Regulations Governing Technology

Article I, Section 8, Clause 8 of the United States Constitution reads:

> The Congress shall have Power To . . . promote the Progress of Science and useful Arts, by securing for limited Times to Authors and Inventors the exclusive Right to their respective Writings and Discoveries;

This clause of the Constitution is the authority by which Congress passed the copyright law of 1972. The copyright law protects the literary, musical, dramatic, pantomimed or choreographed, pictorial, motion picture, sound recording, and architectural works of creative people. Creators have exclusive reproduction, adaptation, distribution, performance, and display rights to their creations. The only requirements of a creative work are that it be the original independent creation of the individual and committed to fixed form. An idea is not copyrightable unless it is developed in fixed form. However, class notes and teachers' lesson plans are copyrightable. Teachers and school administrators who develop writings or PowerPoint presentations have only to include their name, the copyright symbol (©), and the date the work was created to retain rights to the use of their works.

Teachers routinely use multiple copies of written publications and reproduced copies of video recordings as part of their lesson plans. Fair Use provisions of the Copyright Act allow educators a measure of latitude with regard to the use of copyrighted material according to Section 107 of the 1976 Copyright Act.

> . . . the fair use of copyrighted work, including such use by reproduction in copies or phonorecords or by any other means specified by that section, for purposes such as criticism, comment, news reporting, teaching (including multiple copies for classroom use), scholarship, or research, is not an infringement of copyright. In determining whether the use made of a work in any particular case is a fair use the factors to be considered shall include:
>
> 1. the purpose and character of the use, including whether such use is of a commercial nature or is for nonprofit educational purposes;
>
> 2. the nature of the copyrighted work;
>
> 3. the amount and substantiality of the portion used in relation to the copyrighted work as a whole; and
>
> 4. the effect of the use upon the potential market for or value of the copyrighted work.

The specific intent of the Fair Use guidelines was crafted by various groups affected by application of the Copyright Act. In 1976, guidelines that relate to the use of copyrighted books, periodicals, music, and television broadcast materials were addressed. Fair Use Guidelines that address the use of multimedia, digital images, and distance education were developed in 1996.

The 1987 policy Statement on Software Copyright is revised every few years to accommodate an industry that is still evolving. Currently, the owner of a software program is allowed to have a backup copy of the software in case the original disk is damaged or fails to work. Yet, unless the owner of a software program has a license to permit the user to load the contents of one disk into many computers, the Statement on Software Copyright recommends that the user not do so. This policy statement also offers the recommendation that someone obtain a written license agreement from a copyright holder, gaining permission to place a software program on a local area network before doing so. "The 1976 U.S. Copyright Act and its 1980 Amendments remain vague in some areas of software use and its application to education. Where the law itself is vague, software licenses tend to be much more specific. It is therefore imperative that educators read the software's copyright page and understand the licensing restrictions printed there" (Enghagen, 1997, p. 79).

In response to concerns about violations of the Copyright Act by teachers and other school employees, school districts are encouraged to develop district policies that establish clear parameters for use of all technology, including computer software. These policies are usually termed *Internet Acceptable Use* policies, and they include guidelines that require employees to respect copyright and license agreements and cite material.

Application and use of the Copyright Act and education intersect at the copy machine, the video recorder, and, more recently, the computer.

FACTORS TO CONSIDER

- Application of the Copyright Act provisions
- Development of school procedures and policies for use of technology
- Knowledge of penalties for copyright law violations
- Administrator and teacher responsibilities for appropriate use of software

THE CASE

St. Regis School is located in a rural area 25 miles from a large city. The small town of St. Regis has two grocery stores, one drugstore, and a few other small businesses that residents in the surrounding area rely on for basic goods and services. The school in St. Regis serves students of Grades K through 8. When students enter high school, they are transported by bus for a long ride to a high school in the city.

The school's student population of approximately 420 students requires only two teachers in each grade level. One special education teacher serves students of Grades K through 4, while another special education teacher serves children in the upper grades. Financial support for the school, other than the meager state allocation, comes from two major fundraising efforts each year. In the fall, the school sponsors a combination candy and gift wrap sale. In the spring, students ask their parents and relatives to sponsor them in a Spring Fling race and to participate in activities of the PTA-sponsored Spring Fling. The school's annual budget provides basic materials for teachers with a small extra amount dedicated to purchasing either computers or new software.

Mr. Keith Sample has been principal of St. Regis for the past three years. Because he didn't grow up in St. Regis, he worked diligently to establish positive relationships with resistant teachers and longtime residents who didn't accept strangers readily. After his second year as principal, Mr. Sample received feedback from an end-of-the-year survey that he had many more supporters than resistors among the faculty and staff and local residents. He wanted to maintain this status quo, moving toward influencing all to support his vision for St. Regis School.

For the past three years, the PTA and school faculty and staff agreed to use available monies from fundraising to purchase new computers. Because of their efforts, a computer lab housing 20 computers was available to students and teachers. A primary goal agreed on by the parent/faculty committee of the PTA was to purchase new software for the next two years. Consequently, the library/media specialist, Mrs. Lynn, worked with teachers and Mr. Sample to prioritize a list of software programs aligned with the instructional objectives of as many grade levels and subjects as possible.

Mrs. Lynn distributed a form on which teachers submitted to her their requests for software programs. She then worked with Mr. Sample to prioritize the suggested programs for purchase. When this task was accomplished, Mrs. Lynn ordered new software programs for use in the computer lab. The software programs arrived, were catalogued with other emerging technology items, and were stored in the computer lab adjacent to the library for use by teachers and their students. Because the school was relatively small for a K–8 school, the student population didn't support the assignment of a computer lab teacher to the school. Consequently, Mrs. Lynn served as the computer laboratory teacher in addition to her assignment as library/media specialist. She developed a schedule so that each teacher had a scheduled time to use the computer lab for either computer-assisted or computer literacy instruction. All but three of the teachers use the computer lab frequently. Mrs. Lynn is pleased that so many of the teachers make efforts to use the computer lab and to incorporate activities that make maximum use of the new software programs with their units of study.

After four months of following the computer lab schedule, several teachers approached Mrs. Lynn with an idea of how to utilize the new software programs on a broader scale. The teachers wanted to supplement their classroom activities with independent student use of the single computers in their classrooms. They asked Mrs. Lynn to copy the newly purchased software programs so that the programs could be installed on computers in all classrooms. She agreed that having access to these programs in all classrooms would increase student use of the latest technology available in the school. Despite copyright restrictions that govern reproduction of multiple copies without permission from the author, Mrs. Lynn ordered blank CDs for making multiple copies of computer programs selected by teachers to support grade-level objectives. Once copies of computer programs that correlate with third grade objectives were made, Mrs. Lynn distributed the freshly copied CDs to the two third grade teachers, Mrs. Williams, an experienced teacher who has always taught at St. Regis School, and Mrs. Brandon, a teacher new to St. Regis this year. Mrs. Brandon has three years of experience in another school in the northern part of the state.

Mrs. Williams was delighted to receive the copied programs and thanked Mrs. Lynn for her willingness to copy and make purchased computer programs available to all teachers. Mrs. Brandon had a different reaction to the copied computer programs. She explained to Mrs. Lynn that she appreciated her efforts, but that she was concerned about copyright violations. Mrs. Brandon added that teachers were not allowed to make multiple copies of commercial computer programs in her former school. Mrs. Lynn was disgruntled by Mrs. Brandon's remark and responded, "Well, I don't care what you did in your other school, at St. Regis we have to make every penny count for our students!"

At the end of the day, Mrs. Brandon made a point to stop by Mr. Sample's office.

As she entered his office, Mr. Sample said, "What's on your mind, Mrs. Brandon? You look perplexed. Is there a problem?"

"I guess I'm not very good at masking my feelings, Mr. Sample. I am concerned about the way in which Mrs. Lynn is making multiple copies of commercially produced computer programs that are copyrighted. Library/media specialists and teachers weren't allowed to copy purchased programs for one another at my former school. The superintendent was particularly sensitive to violations of the copyright law."

"This is the first I've heard about the copying of computer programs, Mrs. Brandon. Tell me how many and which programs were copied for you by Mrs. Lynn."

"Well, Mr. Sample, I ordered two programs with my instructional allocation funds. Mrs. Williams also used her allocation to purchase two computer programs. Mrs. Lynn made copies of all four programs for all teachers on the second, third, and fourth grade levels. She said that we might want to use the programs for independent center activities. I'm worried, Mr. Sample, because of copyright restrictions. Penalties for knowingly violating copyright laws are pretty severe. I've refused the copies Mrs. Lynn made for me, but the other teachers are using them, and I know about it. What should I do, Mr. Sample? I want to get along with everyone, but I'm uncomfortable with their violation of copyright law."

Mr. Sample made a point to see Mrs. Lynn the next day. He noticed a stack of CDs by a library computer and asked Mrs. Lynn about them. Mrs. Lynn proudly told Mr. Sample that she has found a way to save the school money: "Making multiple copies of the new programs makes the technology available to so many more teachers and students. Our parents worked hard to earn that money, and I've been told that many teachers want to have these programs copied and installed on their classroom computers.

"What's Mrs. Brandon's problem, Mr. Sample? Do I need to call the PTA officers and explain how much money the school will save by copying these expensive and worthwhile programs? Our children deserve the best!"

"You certainly are resourceful," Mr. Sample said, "but I must make you aware that what you are doing is a violation of copyright and will mean serious consequences for the school, the school district, and you if discovered by the publisher. You'll have to collect all copies and stop making others."

"Come on, Mr. Sample," said Mrs. Lynn. "Do you really think anyone will know or care about a few copies for classrooms at St. Regis. We're 25 miles from the closest city. The PTA president, Mrs. Evans, volunteered in the library yesterday. She helped me make the copies and was pleased that we are stretching PTA dollars to help all students and teachers. Based on her comments, other parents want us to continue to use our resources in this way."

Questions

1. What will be the most productive way for Mr. Sample to communicate his position to teachers and Mrs. Evans?

2. How can Mr. Sample minimize tension between Mrs. Lynn and himself?

3. How can principals balance support from parents with interference with school operations?

4. What school policies need to be developed to prevent this situation in the future?

5. Who should Mr. Sample involve in resolving this situation?

Activities

1. Role-play the telephone conservation between Mr. Sample and Mrs. Evans.

2. Outline remarks to address application of the copyright law to the faculty at the next faculty meeting.

3. Draft a local school policy related to use of emerging technologies.

4. Identify key personnel to involve in developing a local school policy related to the use of emerging technologies.

5. Discuss application of the copyright law, including fair use provisions in schools.

ISLLC Standards

STANDARD 5—A school administrator is an educational leader who promotes the success of all students by acting with integrity, fairness, and in an ethical manner.

Knowledge

The administrator has knowledge and understanding of:
- Various ethical frameworks and perspectives on ethics
- The values of the diverse school community

Dispositions

The administrator believes in, values, and is committed to:
- Bringing ethical principles to the decision-making process
- Accepting the consequences for upholding one's principles and actions

Performances

The administrator:
- Demonstrates a personal and professional code of ethics
- Applies laws and procedures fairly, wisely, and considerately

---

STANDARD 6—A school administrator is an educational leader who promotes the success of all students by understanding, responding to, and influencing the larger political, social, economic, legal, and cultural context.

Knowledge

The administrator has knowledge and understanding of:
- The law as related to education and schooling
- Global issues and forces affecting teaching and learning

Dispositions

The administrator believes in, values, and is committed to:

- Recognizing a variety of ideas, values, and cultures
- Importance of a continuing dialogue with other decision makers affecting education

Performances

The administrator facilitates processes and engages in activities ensuring that:

- The school community works within the framework of policies, laws, and regulations enacted by local, state, and federal authorities
- Lines of communication are developed with decision makers outside the school community

REFERENCE

Enghagen, L. K. (1997). *Fair use guidelines for educators.* Northampton, MA: Sterling Publications.

CASE 10

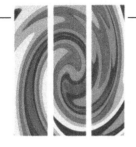

Too Much Parent Involvement!

Organizations Need Boundaries

Effective principals use the school community as a resource to improve programs and strengthen relationships with students. A parent-teacher organization most often serves as the channel through which administrators are able to monitor stakeholders' opinions about the school's successes and areas needing improvement. As Ubben and Hughes (1997) wrote, however, "Nothing good automatically happens just because an organization is labeled in such a way as to suggest a formal relationship with the school" (p. 72). The quality of administrative interactions with parents and students is as important as their frequency.

Parent-teacher organizations should seek their own identity through efforts to improve school programs, but they should retain independence to earn respect from teachers and the rest of the community. An organization that merely endorses administrative decisions without seeking faculty input will lose its credibility. The principal should guide parents to understand the complexity of school programs and their relationship to each other and the budget.

An active parent organization often provides for a large number of volunteers who are willing to work in the school. *With proper training,* they can reduce the number of clerical chores that teachers perform and give teachers more time to spend with instruction and children.

A structured volunteer program fosters effective school-community relations. Parents see firsthand the quality of educational programs and the faculty's dedication to students, but as Lunenburg (1995) reminds us, "no classroom is perfect; the school is society in a microcosm. When we allow adults other than educators in the classroom, we take the chance of them seeing our weaknesses. It is safest to keep our problems to ourselves" (p. 159). Parents' access to classrooms, grade books, and meetings in which faculty discuss students should be limited. New administrators who want to encourage community involvement in school activities should develop volunteer programs that encourage parents to contribute their time and talents, but that access to confidential information that might be misinterpreted and misunderstood by people lacking formal training to work with children in schools.

FACTORS TO CONSIDER

- Planning the use of parent volunteers
- Communication skills
- Community relations
- Confidential student information
- Interpersonal relationship skills

THE CASE

Sheila Massey was content with her elementary supervisor's position until she ran into Dr. Bob Vaughn, a college classmate, at a state curriculum conference. Bob had recently accepted a position as superintendent of Bayside School District.

"Say, Sheila," Bob said during a break in the proceedings, "why don't you think about moving to Bayside? I just received a resignation from an elementary school principal, and from what I remember, you'd be great in that job."

Sheila was flattered but didn't take Bob seriously until he called two weeks after the conference.

"Did you think about my offer?" he asked.

"I didn't know you'd made an offer, Bob," she replied, laughing. "Besides, I like my job here."

Sheila and Bob talked on two other occasions as summer approached. She began to think seriously about leaving her job to become a principal. When she learned three weeks before the end of the term that her position, along with most of the supervisors in her district, was being eliminated because of budget cuts, she phoned Bob.

"Do you still want to interview me for the elementary principal's job?" she asked.

Bob was delighted and encouraged her to submit an application. Her references and credentials were excellent, and she quickly became one of two finalists for the leadership position.

A panel consisting of teachers and parents from Bayside Elementary, a central office supervisor, and the superintendent conducted Sheila's final interview. She felt that she responded to the panel's questions well and made several suggestions about curriculum and teacher evaluations that impressed the committee. They were most receptive to her ideas about volunteers and community involvement.

She was not surprised when Bob called the next day to tell her she had the job.

"The vote was unanimous and the selection committee loved you! They really liked your ideas about getting parents back into the school. That's been a problem at Bayside Elementary for the last few years," he told her.

Sheila promised that she would rent her home and move to an apartment in Bayside within two months. Divorced, she only had to persuade her daughters, both of whom attended the state university, that she had been offered a position she had always wanted.

She moved to Bayside and was pleased with the warm reception she received. Parents and teachers stopped by to give her their best wishes as the first day of school approached.

The year began with Sheila holding meetings with groups of parents and teachers to talk about improving curriculum and to address their concerns. The PTA was especially helpful. Its president, Marjorie Thompson, was Sheila's most ardent supporter.

Marjorie tapped on Sheila's office door one morning and asked for a moment of her time. Sheila was busy working on a budget but set her calculator and financial reports aside.

"Sure, Marjorie, come in."

Marjorie settled into a chair opposite Sheila's desk. "Several mothers want me to ask you if you could use a few volunteers to help out during the day," she said.

"Oh, yes," Sheila replied. "That would be great! I'm sure the teachers would appreciate having volunteers to handle some of their paperwork. I think we could let them work in the faculty lounge. That's a central location, and teachers would know where to find help if they needed it!"

"Good," Marjorie said after she and Sheila talked for several minutes. "I'll announce the news at the next PTA meeting. In the meantime, I'll telephone people who've called and let them know it's all right for them to volunteer. We weren't made to feel welcome before."

Marjorie left and Sheila returned to the budget, believing she had made a wise decision and one that certainly would help to restore the community's confidence in Bayside Elementary School.

During the next five weeks Sheila noticed a marked increase in the number of parents on the campus. Many of them made copies for teachers, decorated bulletin boards, and provided tutorial services to children having difficulty in class. Several volunteers didn't seem to have much to do and remained in the lounge.

Sheila's first hint of trouble came when she received a phone call from the mother of a third grade student to complain that her son, Bobby, had been teased because of a poor math test grade.

"How could any of the other children know what grade Bobby earned?" Sheila asked.

"The teacher lets her volunteer grade papers. Her son is in the class, so I guess she told him about everyone's scores."

Sheila spoke with Bobby's teacher and was assured that she would discontinue the practice of allowing volunteers to grade papers. She hoped the problem was resolved.

A few days later three teachers came to Sheila's office with worried expressions. She sat with them around a small conference table in the corner of the room.

"You look so unhappy," Sheila said. "What's upsetting you?"

The women exchanged glances before Mrs. Thornton, a fourth grade teacher, said, "Ms. Massey, we know you've worked hard to gain public support for the school. Most of us really appreciate what you've done . . ."

"But?" Sheila asked.

"But the volunteers have gotten out of hand," Mrs. Thornton replied. "There are so many of them!"

Sheila listened for 30 minutes as the teachers outlined problems the volunteers had created. Children listened to their mothers rather than their teachers, which made classroom management more difficult than usual; volunteers were taking extra time in the lunch line, which caused afternoon classes to begin late; teachers had no place in which to take a break because the lounge was always filled with parents; and faculty bathrooms were unavailable because volunteers were using them.

After the delegation left, Sheila wondered how to address the issues they had identified. She never thought that a school could have too much community involvement, but the routines she and the faculty had worked hard to instill were being threatened by well-intentioned parents who didn't understand the consequences of their actions.

Sheila decided to discuss the matter with Mrs. Thompson and walked from her office and across the lobby toward the faculty lounge. She noticed a woman sitting on a bench with her head down.

"Excuse me. Are you ill?" Sheila asked as she gently touched the visitor's shoulder.

Dazed, the woman looked into Sheila's face with unfocused eyes. "No . . . I'm fine. I was just taking a nap."

Surprised, Sheila asked, "Are you checking someone out?"

The woman shook her head. "I'm a volunteer, but I haven't had anything to do all day."

Sheila nodded and walked toward the lounge. She heard Mrs. Thompson's laughter as she opened the door.

"Marjorie," she said, "can we talk for a few minutes?"

She knew this was going to be a difficult conversation.

Questions

1. Is Sheila's decision to discuss problems with volunteers with Mrs. Thompson right away a good one? Why or why not?

2. What steps might Sheila have taken to avoid a confrontation with the PTA and its volunteers?

3. Should volunteers have limits on the things they are allowed to do for teachers? Discuss the tasks you believe to be appropriate for parents to perform.

Activities

1. Choose a partner and role-play the conference between Sheila and Mrs. Thompson, the PTA president.

2. Fold a piece of paper so that it contains two columns. In the left-hand column make a list of tasks that you believe volunteers can perform at school. List tasks in which they should *not* be engaged in the right-hand column.

3. Write a letter to Mrs. Thompson that reflects your guidance to her and the PTA for volunteers working in the school.

ISLLC Standards

STANDARD 3—A school administrator is an educational leader who promotes the success of all students by ensuring management of the organization, operations, and resources for a safe, efficient, and effective learning environment.

Knowledge

The administrator has knowledge and understanding of:

- Theories and models of organization and the principles of organizational development
- Operational procedures at the school and district level

Dispositions

The administrator believes in, values, and is committed to:

- Taking risks to improve schools
- Trusting people and their judgments

Performances

The administrator facilitates processes and engages in activities ensuring that:

- Operational procedures are designed and managed to maximize opportunities for successful learning
- Confidentiality and privacy of school records are maintained

---

STANDARD 4—A school administrator is an educational leader who promotes the success of all students by collaborating with families and community members, responding to diverse community interests and needs, and mobilizing community resources.

Knowledge

The administrator has knowledge and understanding of:

- Emerging issues and trends that potentially impact the school community
- Community resources

Dispositions

The administrator believes in, values, and is committed to:

- Schools operating as an integral part of the larger community
- Involvement of families and other stakeholders in school decision-making processes

Performances

The administrator facilitates processes and engages in activities ensuring that:

- The school and community serve one another as resources
- Community stakeholders are treated equitably

REFERENCES

Lunenburg, F. C. (1995). *The principalship: Concepts and applications.* Englewood Cliffs, NJ: Prentice Hall.

Ubben, G. C., & Hughes, L. W. (1997). *The principal: Creative leadership for effective schools.* Boston: Allyn & Bacon.

CASE 11

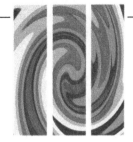

Double Promotion?

Parents Want
Child to Skip a Grade

Providing an instructional program that meets the needs of individual students is one of the greatest challenges faced by classroom teachers and local school principals. A typical class of elementary-age students will be composed of youngsters who range from highly capable students to those who struggle to meet basic grade-level standards. Teachers also are challenged to meet the needs of students who receive special services such as speech pathology, gifted education instruction, or learning disability classes. While some students are motivated by home and school to excel, others are disinterested in academic study and fail to achieve their full academic potential. Daily, teachers are charged with preparing lesson plans that address students' distinct needs, abilities, and levels of motivation for schoolwork. Teachers are called upon to provide activities that accommodate students' different learning styles, modalities, and rates of progress.

Moreover, teachers must interact with parents who hold different expectations for their children. A few parents are never seen at school and fail to respond to correspondence from the teacher. Some parents are pleased for their children to earn average grades and to progress at predictable academic rates of achievement. Such parents typically attend PTA Open House events and schedule conferences with teachers only upon request or when their children experience unusual difficulty with a school assignment. Other parents are dismayed unless their children consistently earn near-perfect scores on all school assignments. Those parents hold high expectations for their offspring and continually monitor their progress on subject matter activities and projects.

State departments of education and local school districts define parameters for student evaluation and assessment through regulations, policies, and instructional practices. Most states develop courses of study listing the objectives and requirements of each grade level/subject matter field. Teachers are accountable for planning appropriate methods to evaluate student progress and to assess levels of understanding of lesson objectives. In fact, the revised evaluation program for teachers requires documentation of methods of evaluation and rates of progress of all students. This process of assessment and evaluation involves

- Aligning curriculum with measures of assessment
- Establishing benchmarks to document mastery
- Communicating expectations to students and parents
- Monitoring progress on daily activities
- Documenting student progress

Aside from federal requirements of the No Child Left Behind Act of 2002, school districts must develop and implement procedures for assigning grades for student coursework. No matter what symbols are used, grading procedures should clearly communicate to students and parents that a student's progress meets grade-level standards, fails to meet grade-level standards, or exceeds grade-level standards.

School districts strive to meet the individual needs of students through special programs and by supporting use of effective instructional practices by teachers. Creative teachers tailor follow-up assignments and activities to challenge students who quickly understand lesson concepts, offer additional activities for students who will benefit from more practice, and provide remedial plans for students who need more time to achieve mastery of lesson objectives. Federal legislation mandates that special services be provided to all students identified as eligible for special education services in specific exceptionalities such as learning disabilities or speech pathology.

When the academic needs of bright students cannot be met through regular instructional practices and innovations, teachers and school administrators must rely on local school policies that govern placement in alternative settings such as gifted education classes or early promotion to a higher grade.

As a group, talented and gifted children tend to learn faster and retain more than their peers. A gifted child is also a divergent thinker. All of these characteristics can be unsettling in a class, and sometimes gifted and talented children have been seen as troublemakers. Other gifted children are turned off by boring classes and become alienated from school (Wiles & Bondi, 2002, p. 239).

Decisions about placement of gifted students also require careful thought and consideration of factors other than a student's academic abilities. Students' social, physical, and emotional development also must be considered. When students are in middle school, differences in their physical and social abilities are greater than when they are in elementary grades. Predicting the best interests of students in future years is a difficult task that requires the collaboration of teachers, school administrators, and parents. When the wishes of parents and the perspectives of school officials differ, conflicts must be resolved.

FACTORS TO CONSIDER

- Implementation of local school district promotion/retention standards
- Instructional practices that meet the individual needs of students
- Collaboration of parents, teachers, and school administrators
- Alternative approaches to student assessment and evaluation
- Instructional assessment of the academic, physical, social, and emotional development of students

THE CASE

As a veteran principal of Twin Oaks Elementary School, David Williams has come to know most students and parents in the school community by name and occupation. The school serves 650 students in Grades K through 5 in a middle-income area of a midsized city. Most parents are high school graduates employed by several factories or industries on the outskirts of the city that specialize in either textiles or machine parts production. A few parents are college or professional school graduates. The student population is composed of diverse and growing populations of Asian and Hispanic students blended with settled populations of both white and black students. Most households are middle-income households with parents who expect that their children will attend college.

At the end of the past school year, Mr. Williams became aware that a group of parents were meeting to discuss the needs of gifted students. Many of these parents had children who were of kindergarten or primary age. After several meetings, they came to see Mr. Williams to discuss the school's plans for meeting the needs of gifted students. They expressed concern that their children were not being challenged to reach their potential. The parents were dissatisfied with the school district's program for academically talented or gifted students. Although an individualized education program (IEP) is developed for each student identified as gifted, instruction with a teacher certified to teach gifted students is limited to one day a week. Regular classroom teachers supplement daily lessons as much as possible. The gifted education teachers serve at least five, and depending on size, sometimes six schools. Because schools in the district have limited classroom space, gifted education teachers are usually assigned to small rooms that serve several purposes, such as textbook storage rooms or portable classrooms separate from main buildings. Without permanent classroom space, gifted education teachers are not able to use bulletin boards that relate to topics of study or to set up center areas for independent exploration. Rarely is equipment such as overhead projectors, computers, or LCD projectors available for use by gifted education teachers. Moreover, gifted education teachers have limited time to confer with regular classroom teachers to correlate instructional objectives in the gifted program with objectives in regular classrooms. Some of the gifted education teachers have complained to parents that funding to purchase supplies and materials for their program has been reduced during the past two years. Parents describe requests to send composition paper, pencils, construction paper, and even calculators to school.

Parents cited many examples of activities and lessons that were geared for average students, with little or no accommodation for gifted students. They presented Mr. Williams with a list of their concerns and submitted a request for special classes that would serve only gifted students. Mr. Williams explained to this group of parents that because of school district financial constraints it was not possible to provide funding for additional teacher units. Moreover, he explained the concern, shared by teachers at the school, that establishing classes to serve only students identified as gifted would limit opportunities for them to interact with the full, diverse population of students enrolled in the school. When Mr. Williams assured parents that he would closely monitor the progress of all academically advanced students, they agreed to forego contacting school board members and the superintendent for the time being.

A particular situation that Mr. Williams has had to confront involves a student new to the school this year whose parents, Mr. and Mrs. Lee, are both attorneys. Last week was the third week of the school year, and Mrs. Wilson, the teacher of Mr. and Mrs. Lee's first grade daughter, Kelly, asked Mr. Williams to review current samples of the child's work. Kelly's work in reading, math, English, and social studies is superior. Mrs. Wilson described Kelly to Mr. Williams as a student who is highly verbal and who has a strong aptitude for understanding abstract mathematical concepts. Her handwriting is neat, but gives evidence of average coordination for a first grade student. Mrs. Wilson added that, while Kelly meets first grade standards of physical agility and balance, she is a shy and withdrawn student who interacts more readily with younger students in kindergarten than with her peers. The teacher told Mr. Williams that Kelly was enrolled in a local preschool from two years of age until she entered kindergarten last year. Mrs. Wilson also described a conference she had with Kelly's parents during the first two weeks of school. At that meeting Kelly's parents told Mrs. Wilson that they felt Kelly's academic needs were not being met. They thought she was bored with first grade work and would be served better academically if she were to be placed in a second grade classroom. Mrs. Wilson disagreed with their recommendation, primarily because, as she stated, Kelly's social development would create problems for her when she reached middle school. Mrs. Wilson felt that Kelly's academic needs would be more effectively met by participation in gifted education classes and enrichment of regular first grade requirements. Undeterred, Kelly's parents explained that their next-door neighbor had a daughter one year older than Kelly and that Kelly's academic abilities surpassed those of the neighbor's child.

Mr. and Mrs. Lee admitted that their daughter was socially ill at ease, even with youngsters her own age; she was also shy and reserved around adults. Kelly's dad acknowledged that his daughter's social development was not as advanced as her academic abilities, but her mom insisted that her academic abilities supported placement in the next grade level. Kelly's mom explained that her daughter's social development did not upset her because she herself was socially immature until she reached high school age. Kelly, she thought, would mature socially in the same way.

Mr. Williams reviewed local school district curriculum policies and procedures that govern student promotion and grade placement. Change in a student's placement to a higher grade at the beginning of a school year requires a recommendation from the assistant superintendent of curriculum and instruction, then approval by the superintendent. If a student is in second grade or above, results of a standardized test are reviewed before a decision is made to promote a student two grades in one year. However, if a student is in first grade or younger, reading and math assessments, in addition to a teacher's recommendation, are the only required criteria to be considered for promoting students to an advanced grade level. Kelly's reading and math assessments documented advanced academic proficiency. Although Mrs. Wilson had reservations about Kelly's social development, she agreed that her academic abilities were highly proficient.

When Mr. Williams spoke with the assistant superintendent of curriculum and instruction, he learned that the school district rarely approved promoting a student two grades in one year. During the past five years, only one other student had been so approved, and that student was an unusually gifted young man. The assistant superintendent of curriculum and instruction cautioned Mr. Williams that if a change were to be made in Kelly's placement, then other parents might petition teachers and the school for similar advancement for their children. As a principal colleague expressed it, "All parents think their children are gifted!"

Mr. Williams has scheduled a conference with Mr. and Mrs. Lee and Mrs. Wilson in one hour. He wants to support the recommendation of the student's teacher. However, when Mr. Lee called Mr. Williams to request a conference, Mr. Lee told Mr. Williams that he and his wife had studied state regulations governing gifted education and local school district promotion/retention standards. While Mr. Lee expressed his respect for Mrs. Wilson's assessment of Kelly's social development, he said that both he and his wife felt that Kelly's academic abilities overshadowed her social skill development. Mr. Lee told Mr. Williams that his brother-in-law, a professor of secondary education at a university in a neighboring state, had recently assessed Kelly's reading ability as fourth grade level. In a friendly but insistent tone, Mr. Lee implied that they intended to use legal measures to have their child placed in a second grade class.

Questions

1. How should Mr. Williams plan to conduct the conference with Mr. and Mrs. Lee?

2. Should other school personnel be involved in this conference?

3. What suggestions do you think will be appropriate to make for Kelly's instructional program?

4. What school district resources will be appropriate to share with Mr. and Mrs. Lee?

5. Should Mr. Williams resolve to support the teacher no matter how adamant Mr. and Mrs. Lee are regarding their request for Kelly's placement in second grade? If not, how would you deal with Mrs. Wilson?

6. What changes in the school program and curriculum, if any, need to be made to support academically capable students?

Activities

1. Draft a memo to Mr. and Mrs. Lee outlining suggestions that will enrich Kelly's program while maintaining her placement in first grade.

2. Draft a memo to the assistant superintendent recommending a change in placement for the student from first to second grade.

3. Role-play a conference with Mr. and Mrs. Lee and Mrs. Wilson.

4. List options for serving Kelly's academic, physical, emotional, and social needs.

5. Develop an agenda to use as a guide for conducting the conference with Mr. and Mrs. Lee.

ISLLC Standards

STANDARD 2—A school administrator is an educational leader who promotes the success of all students by advocating, nurturing, and sustaining a school culture and instructional program conducive to student learning and staff professional growth.

Knowledge

The administrator has knowledge and understanding of:

- Student growth and development
- Applied learning theories
- Measurement, evaluation, and assessment strategies

Dispositions

The administrator believes in, values, and is committed to:

- The variety of ways in which students can learn
- Professional development as an integral part of school improvement
- Preparation of students to be contributing members of society

Performances

The administrator facilitates processes and engages in activities ensuring that:

- Barriers to student learning are identified, clarified, and addressed
- Diversity is considered in developing learning experiences
- Curriculum decisions are based on research, expertise of teachers, and the recommendations of learned societies

STANDARD 5—A school administrator is an educational leader who promotes the success of all students by acting with integrity, fairness, and in an ethical manner.

Knowledge

The administrator has knowledge and understanding of:

- The purpose of education and the role of leadership in modern society
- The values of the diverse school community

Dispositions

The administrator believes in, values, and is committed to:

- The right of every student to a free, quality education
- Using the influence of one's office constructively and productively in the service of all students and their families

Performances

The administrator facilitates processes and engages in activities ensuring that [he or she]:

- Considers the impact of administrative practices on others
- Uses the influence of the office to enhance the educational program rather than for personal gain
- Demonstrates appreciation for and sensitivity to the diversity in the school community

REFERENCE

Wiles, J., & Bondi, J. (2002). *Curriculum development: A guide to practice.* Upper Saddle River, NJ: Merrill Prentice Hall.

CASE 12

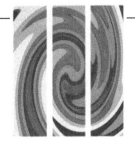

A Problem With Inclusion

Inadequate Resources for Special Education

Nearly two decades have passed since Congress enacted Public Law No. 101-476, the Individuals With Disabilities Education Act (IDEA). Prior to 1991, school districts struggled to teach students with a collection of disorders known as *learning disabilities*. IDEA clarified their condition as "a disorder in one or more of the basic psychological processes involved in understanding or in using language, spoken or written, which may manifest itself in an imperfect ability to listen, think, speak, read, write, spell, or to do mathematical calculations. The term does not include children who have learning problems that are primarily the result of visual, hearing or motor handicaps, of mental retardation, or of environmental, cultural, or economic disadvantage" (Section 5(b)(4)).

According to Hallahan and Kauffman (1994), IDEA prescribed special education's functions as (a) identifying and classifying each case for placement in the appropriate program, (b) mainstreaming each student alongside the "normal" student in school, (c) integrating special education students into society and allowing them to have confidence in their worth as people, and (d) creating an awareness in the school and community of the scope of the exceptional child's problems and of the idea that helping the disabled is a community function.

Special and regular educators collaborated on Individual Education Plans to ensure that disabled students received appropriate services based on diagnostic testing. Those with high-incidence disabilities and labeled as learning disabled were mainstreamed into classrooms with other children for selected subjects, but returned to a resource room with a special education teacher for most of the instructional day.

Mainstreaming was an ineffective compromise. Teachers without special education training experienced difficulty working with special students whose cognitive skills often placed them two or more years behind their peers, but IDEA did not prohibit the procedure and it became the norm in school districts across the nation. It was not uncommon to exclude special education students from annual standardized testing to achieve higher scores since state boards of education evaluated schools based on those tests.

The No Child Left Behind Act (2001) imposed more stringent requirements on schools to include disabled children in regular classrooms on a daily basis. Resource classrooms and mainstreaming continued as alternatives, but the law's provisions that all children must be taught by Highly Qualified teachers and that special and regular education teachers would work cooperatively in the same classroom have made them less attractive options.

The No Child Left Behind Act requires standardized testing of *all* children to ensure that disabled students are receiving an education in the least restrictive environment. They take the same rigorous academic tests as their peers and are represented as a subgroup when results are reported. Administrators must fashion annual plans that identify actions they intend to take to close performance gaps between subgroups.

Lunenburg (1995) reminds administrators that "exceptional children are unlikely to achieve their full human potential without a special education program designed to capitalize on their abilities or help them overcome their disabilities" (p. 241). Some parents of disabled students view categorical labels as stigmatic and refuse the school's consultative or identification services. Administrators must help them to understand the academic and social benefits of matching the school's special education services with a disabled learner's needs.

FACTORS TO CONSIDER

- NCLB's provisions for disabled students
- Inclusive classrooms
- Teacher and parent attitudes about disabled students
- The legality of Individual Education Plans

- Disabled students and Adequate Yearly Progress
- The role of colleges in preparing teachers for inclusive classrooms

THE CASE

"Hello. Is this the principal?" A voice asked. "Yes, ma'am, this is Randy Barnes. How may I help you?"

"My name is Marie Cooley and my son, Steven, will be enrolling in your school in a few days."

"Thanks for letting us know, Mrs. Cooley," Barnes replied. "You should come by the school and pick up a registration packet. What grade will Steven be in?"

"The tenth, but you should know that he's a special education student."

The principal paused. Another special needs student! The faculty at Somerset High was doing its best to understand inclusion, but many teachers continued to resist the idea that teaching students with special needs was their responsibility. Dawn Belle, a member of the English department at Somerset for 20 years and the teachers' union representative, had made the faculty's position clear.

"We didn't sign on to teach *those* kids," she'd said in a faculty meeting two weeks ago. "They take so much of our time that the kids who really want to learn don't have a chance. If I were one of their parents, I'd be up here complaining! They're not getting an equal education!"

Randy had arranged several in-service training sessions to help his teachers understand that inclusion was an effective way to educate special needs students, but he saw little change in their attitude. The majority believed that special education students belonged in a resource room. They continued to believe that the least restrictive environment for disabled children was anywhere but in their classrooms.

"That's fine, Mrs. Cooley," he replied. "We have four excellent special education teachers on our faculty. I'm sure we'll be able to help Steven."

"Well, he's capable of learning, but he's deaf."

Barnes paused. Seventy-three special needs students attended Somerset High, but all of them had either a learning disability or an emotional disorder. Other than two students who used wheelchairs, he'd never enrolled anyone with a physical disability. All campus facilities were accessible, but Randy had assumed that construction to add special toilets, ramps, parking, and door handles was undertaken to comply with federal law.

"I'll be honest, Mrs. Cooley, we've never had a hearing-impaired student . . ."

"No, Mr. Barnes," she interrupted, "not hearing impaired. Steven is deaf!"

The principal glanced at his calendar.

"Can you and Steven come to school for a meeting, Mrs. Cooley? I'd like my special education teachers to meet him. Did he have an IEP [Individual Education Plan] at his last school?"

"Yes," she replied. "I'll bring a copy with me. Steven's always had an interpreter, so you may want to invite your supervisor to the meeting."

Barnes scheduled a meeting with Mrs. Cooley and Steven before phoning Wayne Santos, the district's special education supervisor. Santos agreed to meet and suggested including a counselor and at least one special education teacher in the session. The principal decided to wait until he had met the Cooleys before telling his tenth grade teachers about Steven's disability.

The meeting went well. Steven had been deaf from birth; Mrs. Cooley had devoted much of her life to taking him to one children's hospital after another for surgery that might preserve part of his hearing. As he grew, the structural damage to his inner ears became irreparable. His mother wanted him to have the skills he'd need for a job and to function in society.

Mr. Santos was impressed with Mrs. Cooley's perseverance. She had been discouraged for years by school administrators in efforts to help her son. Most of them suggested in one way or another that Steven would be better off in a school for deaf students. One principal had told her that he couldn't enroll Steven because his district wouldn't provide special education services for hearing-impaired students. Her mention of legal action helped to change his mind.

After Mrs. Cooley left, Mr. Santos, Barnes, Sandra Thomas, one of Somerset's two counselors, and Kathy Watson, a special education teacher, talked about her requests.

"I think we can accommodate Steven's early dismissal two days each week to attend the Speech and Hearing Clinic," Santos observed, "but I don't know where I'm going to find an interpreter who uses American Sign Language."

Barnes shook his head. "I didn't know there were different ways to sign."

"Oh, yes," Mrs. Watson said. "There are several different schools of sign language, but Steven has used American sign all of his life."

"Our local college has a small program to train interpreters," Mrs. Thomas added. "I'll call the Special Education Department to see if it has someone who specializes in American sign. If not, perhaps they might suggest a resource."

"Good idea," Santos nodded. "Mrs. Cooley will enroll Steven next Monday. We've got a lot to do between now and then. We'll certainly want to have another meeting to revise his IEP."

Randy Barnes had another concern. What about Steven's safety during physical education? Even with an interpreter, there were many campus activities that required students to hear what was being said.

"I can't answer that question, Randy. Let's think about our options for a few days," Santos said, bringing the meeting to an end. "Mrs. Thomas, please call the college today and let me know what you find with regard to an interpreter. That's going to be the most difficult part of Steven's IEP."

As everyone stood, Sandra tugged at Randy's coat and motioned for him to stay behind. "What are you going to tell the faculty?" she asked when they were alone in the room. "Steven's in the tenth grade. That means he'll have Mrs. Belle for English, and you know how she feels about special needs students."

Barnes shook his head. "I don't know, Sandra. She doesn't have a choice in the matter, but her attitude about disabled kids makes it difficult for everyone. I'll give the matter some thought tonight and talk with the tenth grade teachers after school tomorrow. Let me know whether or not you have any luck finding an interpreter. That's really important."

Thomas nodded as Barnes returned to his office. She knew gaining the tenth grade teachers' cooperation was going to be difficult.

Questions

1. What will Mr. Barnes say to the tenth grade faculty and to Mrs. Belle about enrolling Steven?

2. Identify possible safety concerns associated with enrolling a deaf child in your school. How will you address each one?

3. What elements *must* be included in a student's Individual Education Plan (IEP)?

4. Are there school activities from which Steven legally can be excluded because of his disability?

5. What is the perception of regular education teachers at your school regarding inclusion and working with special needs students?

Activities

1. Role-play the conference between Mr. Barnes and Mrs. Belle.

2. Discuss the impact that the No Child Left Behind Act and inclusion have on regular education classrooms.

3. As an administrator, discuss the procedures you'll establish to monitor your school's compliance with the provisions of IEPs for special education students.

4. Interview a general education teacher and one who works with disabled students. Compare their opinions about including special education students in regular classes and about the impact standardized tests for everyone are having on learning.

ISLLC Standards

STANDARD 3—A school administrator is an educational leader who promotes the success of all students by ensuring management of the organization, operations, and resources for a safe, efficient, and effective learning environment.

Knowledge

The administrator has knowledge and understanding of:

- Principles and issues related to school safety
- Legal issues impacting school operations

Dispositions

The administrator believes in, values, and is committed to:

- Accepting responsibility
- A safe environment

Performances

The administrator facilitates processes and engages in activities ensuring that:

- Problems are confronted and resolved in a timely manner
- Effective conflict resolution skills are used

STANDARD 6—A school administrator is an educational leader who promotes the success of all students by understanding, responding to, and influencing the larger political, social, economic, legal, and cultural context.

Knowledge

The administrator has knowledge and understanding of:

- The law as related to education and schooling
- The importance of diversity and equity in a democratic society

Dispositions

The administrator believes in, values, and is committed to:

- Education as a key to opportunity and social mobility
- Using legal systems to protect student rights and improve student opportunities

Performances

The administrator facilitates processes and engages in activities ensuring that:

- Communication occurs among the school community concerning trends, issues, and potential changes in the environment in which schools operate
- Public policy is shaped to provide quality education for students

REFERENCES

Hallahan, D. P., & Kauffman, J. M. (1994). *Exceptional children: Introduction to special education* (6th ed.). Boston: Allyn & Bacon.

The Individuals With Educational Disabilities Act (Pub. L. No. 101-476), 5 (b) (4), (1991).

Lunenburg, F. C. (1995). *The principalship: Concepts and applications.* Upper Saddle River, NJ: Merrill Prentice Hall.

CASE 13

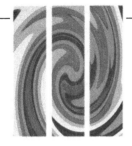

Poor Evaluations for a Teacher

Reassigning an Ineffective Educator

Recent school reform efforts have focused on the principal's leadership skills, but teacher effectiveness has always been an integral part of instructional improvement. Evaluating instruction, identifying teachers' strengths and weaknesses, and providing professional development opportunities constitute an assessment cycle that promotes growth and student learning. Oliva and Pawlas (2004) wrote that "a fully-developed program of teacher evaluation consists of three components: *self-evaluation, formative evaluation,* and *summative evaluation*" (p. 445).

Many school districts use clinical supervision procedures to evaluate their teachers because that method is an objectives-based, formative model designed to foster improvement. Developed in the 1960s to assess student teachers, the model consists of five steps.

Step One: The Pre-observation Conference

The pre-observation conference offers a forum in which the teacher outlines for the principal plans for the lesson to be observed and talks about learning objectives, teaching strategies, resources, and evaluation plans. The principal has an opportunity to clarify the plan and offer suggestions.

Step Two: The Classroom Observation

The teacher's task is to teach the lesson that was discussed with the principal, who records events that occur during the lesson and includes verbal and nonverbal activities. The principal's notes should be objective, not judgmental.

Step Three: Analysis of the Lesson

After observing the lesson, the principal should analyze notes made during the session, paying particular attention to the elements of teaching discussed in the pre-observation conference. A thorough analysis will help to distinguish effective teaching strategies, identify patterns of student and teacher behavior, and find ways in which the teacher may improve.

Step Four: The Post-observation Conference

The teacher and principal meet to talk about the lesson's effectiveness, discuss what went well during the lesson, and review teaching strategies used during the observation to develop a plan for improvement. Specific suggestions should be identified and agreed on.

Step Five: Post-observation Analysis

After the teacher has had a brief period of time to reflect on the principal's suggestions for improvement, specific activities aimed at strengthening weaknesses identified in the lesson should be identified for the teacher's professional development. These usually include suggestions to attend graduate classes, make observations in other schools or classrooms, or attend workshops tailored to the teacher's needs.

There are problems associated with teacher appraisal systems. According to Lunenburg (1995), "Most teachers do not like to be evaluated, and they do not find it helpful to them professionally" (p. 212). He also suggested that their negative feelings may relate more to the manner in which the evaluations are conducted than to the idea of being evaluated, but clinical supervision is designed to attend to their professional needs and improve their teaching abilities.

School districts usually prescribe the instrument that will be used in evaluations, but the knowledge, skills, and dispositions that constitute effective teaching are research based and consistent. Gorton and Schneider (1991) wrote that successful teachers

1. Set high expectations for student achievement

2. Diagnose students' current skills and knowledge before establishing learning objectives and assigning work

3. Set specific learning goals for each lesson

4. Plan thoroughly for each lesson

5. Provide instruction at the appropriate level of difficulty for most students

6. Assign tasks to students based on their ability levels

7. Spend more time on teaching and learning tasks than on administrative work

8. Assess student progress regularly

9. Keep students focused on the task at hand

10. Provide regular feedback to students to promote improvement

11. Reinforce correct student behavior with positive rewards (p. 294)

Teacher efficacy has become important as a result of high-stakes testing in schools. Requirements for Adequate Yearly Progress in the No Child Left Behind Act mean that administrators must know what constitutes effective teaching and help faculty to improve their skills through meaningful professional development activities.

FACTORS TO CONSIDER

- Pre- and post-observation conferences with teachers
- A comprehensive plan to evaluate faculty
- Professional Development Plans
- Communication skills
- Interpersonal relationship skills
- Tenure laws

THE CASE

East LaFayette Middle School was four years old when Ron Altman became its second principal. Altman, an assistant principal in a neighboring district, had become acquainted with Dr. Arthur Allen, the school's first administrator, at regional meetings and conferences. When Dr. Allen was selected to head his district's Human Resources Office, Ron had been interviewed and selected for the vacant position at East LaFayette. Dr. Sandra Rose, the superintendent, wanted administrators with fresh, new ideas, and Ron had impressed her during his interview with ideas about middle school curricula and collaborative decision making.

The position at East LaFayette was challenging. Dr. Allen had hired all 52 of the teachers on staff and was reputed to be a hard, fair boss. Few teachers sought transfers from the school. Ron interviewed new faculty as enrollment continued to increase. Most applicants came from inside the district.

The school surpassed its academic goals and enjoyed the community's support. Altman envisioned East LaFayette's earning national recognition for its accomplishments, but he wanted to wait a year or two before going through the rigorous application process.

Ron's ideas about instructional leadership took him to teachers' classrooms regularly. He completed the district's mandated observation forms but set a personal goal of visiting three classes each day for 30 minutes. He enjoyed a good relationship with teachers and students, many of whom respectfully called him "Mr. A." They described him as fair and as a good listener.

On a warm Tuesday in July between his third and fourth years at LaFayette, Ron answered the telephone and heard Dr. Allen's voice.

"Hey, Ron, how's the summer going?"

"Fine, Arthur," Altman replied. "Are you calling to tell me you found a seventh-grade math teacher?"

"Sort of," Allen's voice trailed off. "I'm transferring a math teacher to you from Jemison Middle."

"That doesn't sound too bad. Who is it?"

"Her name's Anna Richardson, Ron. She's had some problems at Jemison."

Altman paused. This was unusual. Allen usually sent names of candidates to principals, who conducted their own interviews and recommended the applicant they wanted to hire.

Ron leaned back in his chair. "Why are you sending her here if she's having problems? I'm trying to build something . . ."

"I know, Ron, I know," Allen said. "Dr. Rose decided that she's received enough complaints about Ms. Richardson. She's tenured and the only way we can fire her is to do a better job documenting her problems."

"Arthur, you're sending me a problem teacher because Dr. Rose wants me to get rid of her?"

"Look, Ron, I don't know Ms. Richardson. Her file is thick with letters from parents complaining about her. There are lots of observation reports from supervisors and principals, but no one was willing to dismiss her. I'm sorry, but she's going to be assigned to your school. If you think it'd help, stop by the office and review her file."

After he hung up the phone, Ron considered what he'd been told. He knew Dr. Allen had no choice about assigning Ms. Richardson to East LaFayette Middle. At least he'd called with a warning. Altman wondered what he'd say to his faculty. He relied on them to help with interviews; they'd be surprised when Ms. Richardson arrived.

Altman decided to call Tyra Wright at Jemison Middle. She'd been the principal there for a few years and had always impressed Ron as hardworking and competent.

"Hello, Tyra," he said when she answered on the second ring. "This is Ron Altman."

"I know why you're calling, Ron, and I'm so sorry. I just didn't know what else to do, so I spoke with Dr. Rose. It was her decision to transfer Ms. Richardson."

"I know, Tyra. I'm not blaming you. I'm trying to figure out the best way to manage the problem. Tell me about Ms. Richardson."

Ms. Wright took 15 minutes to describe problems she'd had with the teacher. Parents and students complained often and loudly. Two members of the board of education had visited her classroom in response to calls they'd received.

"That's about it, Ron," Ms. Wright said. "She was the weakest geography teacher I've ever had and she just wasn't making satisfactory progress."

"Wait a moment, Tyra," Altman said. "Did you say geography?"

"Why, yes. She's certified to teach geography and math, but I didn't need a math teacher when she was transferred to me. Let me check something," she said, setting the telephone on her desk.

"Yes, that's what I thought," Wright said when she returned. "Ms. Richardson completed her fourth year at Jemison, but she's always taught geography or social science. She was a math major, but hasn't ever taught math."

Altman rubbed his chin. "Thanks, Tyra. I think I'll invite Ms. Richardson in for a meeting. It's time for us to talk."

"Good luck, Ron," Wright said as she hung up.

Altman stood and walked to a window overlooking the school's parking lot. He didn't like having a teacher assigned to the faculty without his approval, but there wasn't anything he could do about that. That had been Dr. Rose's decision.

He returned to his chair and reached for the telephone. He wanted to meet Ms. Richardson but wasn't certain about what to say to her.

"Hello, Ms. Richardson? This is Ron Altman, the principal at East LaFayette Middle School. You've been transferred to my faculty, and I thought we should meet and talk about your assignment. When can you come to the school?"

Questions

1. Should Mr. Altman review Ms. Richardson's personnel file before he meets her? Why or why not?

2. How are interviews for teachers conducted at your school? How would you change the process of selecting teachers?

3. Anecdotal notes about a teacher's performance should include several elements. What are they?

4. What will you say to your faculty about Ms. Richardson's assignment to the school?

Activities

1. Role-play the meeting between Mr. Altman and Ms. Richardson.

2. After the meeting, write a letter or memorandum to Ms. Richardson specifying the level of professional performance you expect from her.

3. Discuss the personnel issues pertinent to this case study. What influence does tenure have on a teacher's performance? Did Dr. Allen behave ethically in making the decision to transfer an ineffective teacher to East LaFayette Middle School? If not, what should he have done?

4. Role-play a meeting between you and two or three faculty members during which you explain Ms. Richardson's assignment to your school.

5. To what grade and subject will you assign the new teacher? Why?

ISLLC Standards

STANDARD 5—A school administrator is an educational leader who promotes the success of all students by acting with integrity, fairness, and in an ethical manner.

Knowledge

The administrator has knowledge and understanding of:

- Various ethical frameworks and perspectives on ethics
- Professional codes of ethics

Dispositions

The administrator believes in, values, and is committed to:

- Subordinating one's own interest to the good of the school community
- Accepting the consequences for upholding one's principles and actions

Performances

The administrator:

- Demonstrates values, beliefs, and attitudes that inspire others to higher levels of performance
- Treats people fairly, equitably, and with dignity and respect

---

STANDARD 6—A school administrator is an educational leader who promotes the success of all students by understanding, responding to, and influencing the larger political, social, economic, legal, and cultural context.

Knowledge

The administrator has knowledge and understanding of:

- The law as related to education and schooling
- Models and strategies of change and conflict resolution as applied to the larger political, social, cultural, and economic contexts of schooling

Dispositions

The administrator believes in, values, and is committed to:

- Education as a key to opportunity and social mobility
- Importance of a continuing dialogue with other decision makers affecting education

Performances

The administrator facilitates processes and engages in activities ensuring that:

- The environment in which schools operate is influenced on behalf of students and their families
- The school community works within the framework of policies, laws, and regulations enacted by local, state, and federal authorities

REFERENCES

Gorton, R., & Schneider, G. (1991). *School-based leadership: Challenges and opportunities* (3rd ed.). New York: McGraw Hill.

Lunenburg, F. C. (1995). *The principalship: Concepts and applications.* Upper Saddle River, NJ: Merrill Prentice Hall.

Oliva, P. F., & Pawlas, G. E. (2004). *Supervision for today's schools* (7th ed.). Hoboken, NJ: John Wiley & Sons.

CASE 14

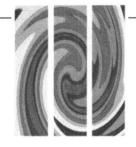

Missing Booster Club Funds

Athletic Funds Are Missing

Have you ever heard the statement, "Ineffective leadership skills result in recommendations for improvement, but mishandling of financial matters results in dismissal"? Well, it's true. Questionable accounting practices draw attention when uncovered, whereas ineffective leadership skills are addressed only in ways to bring about improvement.

School accounts must be maintained in accordance with generally accepted accounting principles and be satisfactorily reviewed by an independent licensed accountant on an annual basis. School accounting procedures must satisfy a principal's obligation to ensure compliance with the legal, regulatory, and fiduciary responsibilities of his or her position of public trust. Funds received and funds expended must be accounted for according to principles adopted by the school board of the district in which the principal is working. Formal procedures for financial accounting may differ from one district to another, but no matter what system a school board elects to follow, principals must ensure that accounting procedures are followed by all personnel and by parents who assume leadership roles in school-sponsored organizations.

Principals must also monitor cash accounting by parent volunteers who work with groups such as the Parent Teacher Association (PTA) or an athletic booster club because principals have responsibility for funds generated by school or student activities. "In general, specific procedures must be established to control the collection and disbursement of the variety of activity funds" (Ubben, Hughes, & Norris, 2004, p. 287). Working with the school book-keeper, principals must follow established procedures for handling all fund accounts, including the general fund, cafeteria fund, and booster club funds. Most school boards take measures to have local school principals and book-keepers bonded by a bonding agency as insurance that public monies mis-appropriated or embezzled will be insured and can be recovered by the school district.

> One area of school accounting that requires close supervision is that of school-sponsored activity funds, which are established to account for monies received from extracurricular activities. Student activity funds deserve special consideration because they are so often neglected and poorly managed, particularly monies derived from extra class fees, athletic con-tests, plays, concerts, sales, and special programs of all kinds. From these sources, many thousands of dollars may be handled each year, even in a small school; in the large school system, the figure easily reaches six dig-its. (Drake & Roe, 2003, p. 462)

Extracurricular activities complement the curriculum, but they operate inde-pendently of the instructional program offered students. Often, receipt of funds through extracurricular activities involves students or parent volunteers in the handling of cash. Parent volunteers often receive and count cash when candy or gift-wrap sales are sponsored by a PTA. Students and parents handle cash receipts when they serve as gatekeepers for athletic events at the high school and middle school levels or assist with concessions for athletic or other school-sponsored events. The character of these types of activity funds makes them particularly vulnerable to mishandling or theft. Internal control procedures designed to safeguard money collected for student activities are critical, because considerable sums of money are collected in the form of currency.

Safeguards for handling activity funds include measures such as reporting all activity funds in the school's financial statements and developing an account-ing trail for all monies collected. Cash receipts and admission tickets can be prenumbered to determine the total amount collected. Volunteer assignments should be changed often. The people who collect money for athletic events or concessions should be rotated so that no one is allowed to collect money for the same event on a regular basis. Unless a school has a small staff and few vol-unteers, two people should be assigned to collect admissions: One person can sell tickets, which are then collected by the other person.

This case study will focus on an instance of theft by a parent volunteer col-lecting admission proceeds from a school athletic event. A typical procedure for handling cash receipts is for the school bookkeeper to prepare a cash box for use by the gatekeeper. The bookkeeper provides small bills and coins that may be used as change when participants present the gatekeeper with large bills. An accounting sheet is included with the cash box to document how much of each paper bill denomination and how many coins of each value are placed in the cash box before the athletic event. At least two people verify with signatures the beginning amount of cash placed in the cash box. During the athletic event, the gatekeeper(s) collects proceeds from admissions and makes change when necessary. At the end of the athletic event, the gate proceeds are counted and at least two people verify with signatures the ending amount of cash collected in the cash box. After the athletic event, the cash is deposited in the night depository at the bank, and accounting paperwork is submitted to the school bookkeeper as soon after the athletic event as possible.

Extracurricular activity fund accounts are included and reported in the school's budget just as are curricular fund accounts. When the school's funds are audited, these accounts must balance just as all other accounts must balance. Paperwork to support the receipt and disbursement of funds from activity accounts must be kept in order and accurately reflect the monies collected and spent. Responsibility for accurately maintaining activity funds is a significant one for principals because of the number of people involved in collecting monies and because the money is collected as currency as opposed to checks. It behooves school principals and assistant principals to follow school board procedures for handling activity fund accounts and to establish local safeguards in line with recommendations from the Association of School Business Officials (ASBO).

FACTORS TO CONSIDER

- Administrative responsibility for safeguarding and maintaining activity fund accounts
- Public relations with parent groups
- Knowledge of business management practices and procedures
- Selection of parent leadership for parent organizations and athletic booster clubs

THE CASE

Located in the middle of an old residential area of the large city of Warren, George Washington Middle School serves approximately 450 students, a relatively small size for a middle school. The student population is declining because younger couples are moving to suburban areas adjacent to the city. Over the past 10 years, not only has the student population at George Washington declined; the socioeconomic level of families has decreased as well. Families served by the school don't have the resources to move to the suburbs; most parents work at a textile mill in the industrial park of Warren.

Despite changes in student population and socioeconomic levels of families at George Washington, community involvement remains strong. Working and nonworking parents frequently volunteer to support school activities. The school's PTA has a list of parents available to help with after-school events, and a few are able to schedule time during the day to participate in a *Reading Buddies* program for middle school students and to collect and count proceeds of PTA fundraisers.

Students participate in three districtwide sports activities: basketball, volleyball, and track. Tryouts for eight cheerleader positions are held each spring. Parents of student athletes and cheerleaders regularly volunteer to collect gate proceeds and to sell concessions at athletic events. The Booster Club president requests the help of four parent volunteers to work each athletic event. Two parents manage concessions, while two other parents collect and monitor gate proceeds.

Daniel Stevens is the current principal at George Washington Middle School. He was appointed four years ago and is well liked by students, parents, and teachers. Mr. Stevens works well with parent leadership in the PTA and the Booster Club. Because he doesn't have an assistant principal to help him with extra duty assignments, such as supervising athletic events, Mr. Stevens relies on parent volunteers to attend and assume responsibility for duties at athletic events.

One of the parents who often volunteers to either manage concessions or collect gate proceeds is Mrs. Alice Bowman. Mrs. Bowman has three children—two sons who have completed middle school and moved on to the high school and one daughter who is a seventh grade cheerleader at George Washington. In fact, Lucy, the daughter, is quite skilled in cheerleader stunts and routines. She was recognized as an All-State cheerleader at the recent tryouts held at the major state university. In addition to receiving a plaque and certificate of accomplishment, Lucy has been invited to march with other All-State cheerleaders in a holiday parade in New York. Mr. Stevens proudly reported Lucy's accomplishments schoolwide one morning during his daily school announcements.

The Thursday following Lucy's participation in the All-State cheerleader tryouts, Mrs. Bowman made an appointment to speak with Mr. Stevens. She arrived on time and explained that she and her husband wanted to request that the PTA fund Lucy's trip to New York. Mrs. Bowman had investigated necessary expenses and presented a budget of $798 needed to purchase an airline ticket, pay for a hotel room shared with four other All-State cheerleaders from other states, and cover meals for three days.

Mr. Stevens reviewed the budget presented by Mrs. Bowman and then explained that he could not support her request. He tactfully stated that while he valued Lucy's contributions to the cheerleading squad and also was proud of her accomplishments, he didn't feel it appropriate for the PTA to expend limited resources on behalf of only one student. Mr. Stevens told Mrs. Bowman that PTA monies were raised to support projects that would benefit all or the majority of students. He justified his position by asking Mrs. Bowman how she might feel if PTA monies were used to send only one student to a summer academic camp. Mrs. Bowman pressed Mr. Stevens to reconsider, but he was adamant that her request was outside the parameters of a legitimate PTA-supported project.

The next time Mr. Stevens saw Mrs. Bowman was Monday night at the last home basketball game of the season for George Washington Middle School. The crowd was large and met seating capacity of the bleachers. Volunteers collecting gate proceeds and concessions worked feverishly to accommodate the crowd. Mr. Stevens was fully occupied with supervisory duties and unable to oversee money collection and accounting. He reasoned that reliable parents and careful accounting procedures made it unnecessary for him to closely supervise parent volunteers. Mr. Stevens knew that prenumbered tickets and an inventory of concession items made it difficult for funds to be mishandled. He wouldn't have had reason for concern had it not been for Mr. Will Dumas.

Mr. Dumas arrived at the game toward the end of the first quarter. He was a foreman at the textile mill and had cashed his weekly check that afternoon. As he approached the door to the gym, he folded several bills to place in his wallet.

"I can see you're doing well, Mr. Dumas," Mr. Stevens said standing at the gym door.

"Yeah, I just got paid and had to use a $50 bill to pay my way to the ball game tonight," Mr. Dumas responded.

"That's great," said Mr. Stevens. "We'll take whatever denomination you have, because we're glad to see you here for the last game of the season. It's going to be a good one!"

After the game, Mrs. Bowman handed Mr. Stevens the bank bag with the door proceeds. He secured the gym and took both the ticket and concession bank bags to his car. The security guard walked with him because Mr. Stevens always arranged for security to accompany him to the bank to make the deposit. Following his usual routine, Mr. Stevens opened the concession money bag and counted it in front of the security guard. The concession money balanced with the inventory and was in order. Mr. Stevens then reviewed the ticket accounting sheet before counting ticket proceeds. Mrs. Bowman had written a note stating that tickets 78 though 88 had to be discarded because they were torn. The ticket proceeds balanced with the number of tickets sold minus the 10 reported torn, but the total didn't reflect the amount that should have included the 10 tickets Mrs. Bowman claimed were torn. Mr. Stevens couldn't find a $50 bill, the cost of 10 tickets, among the currency in the bank bag.

Questions

1. What steps should Mr. Stevens take to determine the whereabouts of the $50 bill?

2. Whom should Mr. Stevens involve in the investigation of this discrepancy?

3. How can Mr. Stevens balance positive relationships with parents while investigating the missing $50 bill and 10 torn tickets?

4. What will be the school bookkeeper's responsibility toward resolving this situation?

5. How will you propose selecting parents to help with money receipt and accounting in the future?

Activities

1. Discuss measures in your school district to safeguard monies collected through school activity events.

2. Role-play the conference between Mr. Stevens and Mrs. Bowman relating to her request for PTA funding to support her daughter's trip to New York.

3. Outline a plan to monitor parent volunteer participation in school activities.

4. Draft a memo to the superintendent describing your concerns about the ticket proceeds accounting.

5. Develop an agenda for a parent volunteer orientation.

ISLLC Standards

STANDARD 3—A school administrator is an educational leader who promotes the success of all students by ensuring management of the organization, operations, and resources for a safe, efficient, and effective learning environment.

Knowledge

The administrator has knowledge and understanding of:

- Operational procedures at the school and district level
- Principles and issues relating to fiscal operations of school management

Dispositions

The administrator believes in, values, and is committed to:

- Trusting people and their judgments
- Involving stakeholders in management processes

Performances

The administrator facilitates processes and engages in activities ensuring that:

- Organizational systems are regularly monitored and modified as needed
- Effective problem-framing and problem-solving skills are used

---

STANDARD 4—A school administrator is an educational leader who promotes the success of all students by collaborating with families and community members, responding to diverse community interests and needs, and mobilizing community resources.

Knowledge

The administrator has knowledge and understanding of:

- The conditions and dynamics of the diverse school community
- Community relations and marketing strategies and processes

Dispositions

The administrator believes in, values, and is committed to:

- Families as partners in the education of their children
- An informed public

Performances

The administrator facilitates processes and engages in activities ensuring that:

- A comprehensive program of community relations is established
- Public resources and funds are used appropriately and wisely

REFERENCES

Drake, T. L., & Roe, W. H. (2003). *The principalship* (6th ed.). Upper Saddle River, NJ: Merrill Prentice Hall.

Ubben, G. C., Hughes, L. W., & Norris, C. J. (2004). *The principal: Creative leadership for excellence in schools* (5th ed.). Boston: Pearson Education.

CASE 15

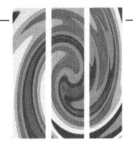

Mentoring New Teachers

A Transition to the Classroom

In Homer's *Odyssey,* Odysseus asks his friend, Mentor, to guide his son, Telemachus, while Odysseus is away on a trip. *Mentor* has come to mean one person guiding another. According to Matthews and Crow (2003), mentoring "is an act of advocacy . . . the support and development of a new teacher are highly moral acts of leadership" (p. 253).

School administrators must remember that new teachers are unfamiliar with the role expectations of their position and need as much detailed information as they can receive. Mentors should be assigned from the same school, grade or department, and subject area and be willing to give nonjudgmental advice. Gorton and Schneider (1991) wrote that in addition to a clear role definition, beginning teachers need assistance with (a) planning and organizing for teaching, (b) motivating and evaluating students, (c) controlling and disciplining students, (d) establishing friendly and cooperative relationships with other members of the school or district, (e) communicating with parents and the community, and (f) achieving personal and professional self-confidence.

Another consideration for administrators is to understand that mentoring consists of more than a meeting in which new teachers receive their class rolls and a copy of the faculty handbook. The process of guiding a novice through the initial stages of a career may take more than one year. Considering the shortage of qualified teachers many school districts face today, investing in resources to develop mentoring programs might help retain new teachers beyond their third year, the time when more than 50 percent of them resign. Other data suggest that mentoring reduces faculty turnover and burnout leading to attrition.

Developing new teachers involves ethical acts of leadership that principals should take seriously. Matthews and Crow (2003) noted that, "Unfortunately, this responsibility is too often neglected or abdicated by principals" (p. 80), who believe credentials from a reputable teacher education program and good marks in student teaching are sufficient to launch the newcomer successfully into a classroom and a career.

The real work of helping new teachers begins *after* they have been recruited, interviewed, and hired. The principal's or assistant principal's most important task in mentoring is to provide visible signs of support to beginning teachers during their first year. New teachers appreciate the help they receive from peers, but they expect assistance from administrators.

The problems about which new teachers complain and the discouragement they feel are attributable to more than command of the subject matter they teach. Linda Darling-Hammond (1984) found that new teachers are "pressured by class size and diversity, management considerations, failure to master subject content, and the inability to assimilate into the culture of the school environment" (p. 27). The principal's role in allocating resources (i.e., funds, classrooms, assigning students to classes, support with discipline problems) will determine the kind of year a new teacher will have.

Oliva and Pawlas (2004) suggest that "master teachers and mentors will help induct beginning teachers into the profession" (p. 530). Mentors guide protégés to examine their perspectives on teaching, students, discipline, and other professional responsibilities through active, open-minded discussions. These conferences may occur on a scheduled basis or when a mentor and new teacher believe they have issues to discuss.

Crow and Matthews (1998) developed four guidelines to help mentors during reflective conferences: (1) Engage in active listening, (2) refrain from judgment and offering too much advice, (3) ask insightful questions, and (4) brainstorm alternative approaches (p. 85). During these conferences a mentor has opportunities to share past experiences that invite comparisons and reflective thinking by a new teacher. Regardless of the issues discussed, the conference's objectives are to increase student learning and to improve teacher professional development.

Principals who want to develop a mentoring program should consider two procedures. The first involves establishing and maintaining a collegial and supportive environment in which beginning teachers have several mentors. The second is based on the principal's selection of a veteran teacher who is willing and qualified to mentor. The second approach usually can be established more quickly than the first, but both require planning and special effort by the principal.

The success of mentoring is related to the amount of time beginning teachers spend with their mentors. Principals should consider the number of subject preparations, types of courses, schedule, duty assignments, and district requirements on new teachers as they recruit and train mentors. Matthews and Crow (2003) remind administrators that beginning teachers are less interested in extrinsic rewards than in being released from at least some obligations in order to engage in mentoring activities. Reducing their load gives them the time and energy to be effective partners in the mentoring process (p. 93).

FACTORS TO CONSIDER

- Selecting and training mentors
- Recruiting and retaining teachers
- Inducting new teachers
- Enhancing communication skills
- Engaging in reflective discussions
- Giving instructional and extra-duty assignments to new teachers

THE CASE

Barbara Felton glanced at her watch. Both of the new teachers she had hired three weeks ago would arrive in 20 minutes for an orientation.

Barbara's 10th year as principal would begin in three weeks. This was the busiest time of the summer, but she believed that nurturing beginning teachers was everyone's job, and she liked to orient them to the school and explain her expectations before the year began.

Barbara remembered her own first-year experience. She'd been given a key, a calendar, and a handshake. Her principal had explained that good teachers showed initiative and asked someone when they wanted to know something. She had felt so overwhelmed!

Felton decided that she'd never treat new teachers that way. She believed they needed more help, not less, and had worked hard to develop the program with her faculty to help beginning teachers succeed.

Barbara believed that teachers did a better job in the classroom if they felt comfortable and self-assured in their surroundings. They needed a friendly face and a kind voice to help them through the first trying months of school. It had become especially important to help new teachers succeed since there weren't enough applicants to fill the vacancies in her district, and finding special education teachers had become impossible!

"Your new teachers just arrived," the school secretary announced as she stepped into the principal's office. "They're coming up the sidewalk now."

"Thanks," Barbara replied. "We'll meet in the cafeteria. Mrs. Phillips will be here soon; please send her in. I want her to meet Ms. Kowalski."

The secretary nodded and left the office. Barbara followed her and walked to the lobby where Sharon Kowalski, a third grade teacher, and Ed Zimmer, certified to teach special needs students, waited.

Barbara led the teachers on a tour of the campus, pointing out the gymnasium, library, playground, and faculty restrooms and lounge and the classrooms to which they would be assigned. They were enthusiastic and asked lots of questions. Mr. Zimmer was curious about inclusion classes at Twin Oaks.

"Let's talk about that when we return to the cafeteria. Honestly, Mr. Zimmer, my faculty is confused about how we can include our disabled students into regular classes."

They returned to the cafeteria, where Barbara had coffee and pastries waiting for them.

"Are those ours?" Ms. Kowalski asked, pointing at two stacks of papers on a table.

"Yes," Felton nodded. "Let's take our coffee to the table and we'll get started."

Barbara took 10 minutes to explain that being recruited, interviewed, and hired was only the beginning of their induction experience. She said that her goal was to help them to have such a successful year at Twin Oaks that they would want to return.

"The next step is to give you an orientation to the school. I know you have a meeting in the central office later this week. Lots of people will tell you about the district and what the system expects of you, but this is where you'll teach every day, so I want to welcome you to *our* school," she smiled.

"Ms. Kowalski," Felton continued, "I've asked Karen Phillips to be your mentor this year. She's been a third grade teacher for eight years."

"Did she have a successful first year?" Zimmer asked, smiling.

"Yes, I think she did, and she had a mentor, too. I want you to think of your mentor as someone to whom you can turn when you have questions about what you're doing with students, or how the school operates, or any other concerns. You certainly may ask me, but sometimes teachers feel better talking to other teachers. The mentoring process will continue throughout the year and involves several planned meetings and discussions so you can ask questions."

"Will I have a mentor?" Zimmer asked.

Felton smiled. "Yes, you will. In fact, you'll have two. Judy O'Hearn is a special education teacher and has been trained to be a mentor."

"Who's the other one?"

"I'll be the other, Mr. Zimmer, because I think we can learn from each other. I want to know more about inclusion, and I can help you to work with the faculty."

"Fair enough," Zimmer nodded.

"Good. Shall we begin?"

As they seated themselves, Barbara removed the top page from the materials on the table and placed it in front of them.

"This is an Orientation Agenda," she said as she gave each one a piece of paper. "As we discuss each item, please check it off. You'll see a place for your signature at the bottom of the page. Please sign the agenda and give it to me before you leave."

She waited while the new teachers previewed the page.

Questions

1. What items should be included on the Orientation Agenda?

2. Does your school have a mentoring program for new teachers? What skills do you think an effective mentor should have?

3. What are the advantages of a principal serving as a mentor for a new teacher? The disadvantages?

Activities

1. What percentage of new teachers resign within three years of taking their first position? Within five years? Why do you think pre-tenure resignation rates are so high?

2. After you become an administrator, what can you do to make teaching attractive to beginners?

3. Assume that you recently discussed the need for a mentoring program with your faculty and several veteran teachers expressed interest in participating. Develop an agenda for your first session. Include your reasons for the program, the skills you think mentors need, and a schedule of the first year's activities for mentors and protégés.

4. List rewards or incentives you can offer mentors to sponsor new teachers.

5. Interview a teacher who was mentored to learn about the benefits of a mentoring program. Interview another who didn't have a mentor. Ask them to talk about their first few years of teaching and compare their answers.

ISLLC Standards

STANDARD 2—A school administrator is an educational leader who promotes the success of all students by advocating, nurturing, and sustaining a school culture and instructional program conducive to student learning and staff professional growth.

Knowledge

The administrator has knowledge and understanding of:

- Adult learning and professional development models
- The change process for systems, organizations, and individuals

Dispositions

The administrator believes in, values, and is committed to:

- Professional development as an integral part of school improvement
- A safe and supportive learning environment

Performances

The administrator facilitates processes and engages in activities ensuring that:

- There is a culture of high expectations for self, student, and staff performance
- Professional development promotes a focus on student learning consistent with the school vision and goals

---

STANDARD 3—A school administrator is an educational leader who promotes the success of all students by ensuring management of the organization, operations, and resources for a safe, efficient, and effective learning environment.

Knowledge

The administrator has knowledge and understanding of

- Theories and models of organizations and the principles of organizational development
- Operational procedures at the school and district level

Dispositions

The administrator believes in, values, and is committed to:

- Making management decisions to enhance learning and teaching
- Taking risks to improve schools

Performances

The administrator facilitates processes and engages in activities ensuring that:

- Operational procedures are designed and managed to maximize opportunities for successful learning
- Operational plans and procedures to achieve the vision and goals of the school are in place

REFERENCES

Crow, G. M., & Matthews, L. J. (1998). *Finding one's way: How mentoring can lead to dynamic leadership.* Thousand Oaks, CA: Corwin Press.

Darling-Hammond, L. (1984). Taking the measure of excellence: The case against basing teacher evaluations on student test scores. *American Educator: The Professional Journal of the American Federation of Teachers, 8*(3), 26–29, 46.

Gorton, R. A., & Schneider, G. T. (1991). *School-based leadership: Challenges and opportunities* (3rd ed.). New York: McGraw-Hill.

Matthews, L. J., & Crow, G. M. (2003). *Being and becoming a principal: Role conceptions for contemporary principals and assistant principals.* Boston: Pearson Education.

Oliva, P. F., & Pawlas, G. E. (2004). *Supervision for today's schools* (7th ed.). Hoboken, NJ: Wiley/Jossey-Bass.

CASE 16

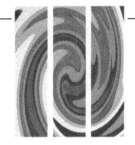

A Gift for the Principal

"Fringe" Benefits?

Local school principals have responsibility for many types of business management functions. They work with the school bookkeeper to follow procedures for fund accounting, they are required to maintain accurate records of all purchases made by school professional and support personnel, and they shoulder responsibility for materials management. In addition to office accounting, principals in schools that have lunch or lunch and breakfast programs also supervise cafeteria accounting. Although not an approved policy, an unspoken but established rule is that cafeteria accounts maintain funds for at least two months of operating expenses. Special procedures or bid laws define parameters for purchases that exceed specified amounts such as an expensive piece of equipment for the cafeteria or a copy machine for the teachers' workroom. When such a purchase is necessary, the bid process is followed to identify the item that meets specifications for the product and is available at the lowest price. When specifications for the product are met, additional features can be considered to justify awarding the bid to a higher bidder. The bid process is required for purchases at school sites as well as for purchases made at the central office level.

Because governance of education rests at the state and not the federal government level, management of school funds is governed by state law, state board of education regulations, and local school district policies. School principals are obligated to know and to follow business management practices required by their states and local districts. A key point for principals to understand is that school funds are public monies, and the public has the right to ask questions and request information related to budgets and management of school funds.

Until the mid-1980s, many principals made independent decisions with respect to school financial matters. In recent times, the site-based philosophy of school management has shifted responsibility from the principal alone to the principal working with a group of school and community people. Some principals may be required to appoint a budget committee. Other principals involve appropriate personnel when the budgeting process or a financial operation is pertinent to their function. Regardless of the structure used to include faculty, staff, and parents in the financial matters of the school, principals are expected to solicit input from others.

Another expectation of principals is to meet standards of ethics adopted by state boards of education and by professional organizations such as the American Association of School Administrators (AASA). Standards that typically are included in ethics codes relate to professional conduct, trustworthiness, unlawful acts, public funds and property, and remunerative conduct. More specifically, ethical conduct includes insuring that institutional privileges are not used for personal gain. Principals are expected to maintain integrity with businesses when accepting gifts, gratuities, favors, or additional compensation. Accepting gifts from vendors or potential vendors for personal use or gain where there appears to be a conflict of interest is an example of a practice that is an ethics violation and sometimes a violation of state law.

In the early days of the 21st century, news commentators reported on numerous instances of elected officials and business leaders who had personally profited from improper relationships with lobbyists or other interests who sought to curry favor. These news stories have heightened the sensitivities of parents and educators to public figures who administer financial responsibilities in questionable ways. Moreover, these instances have challenged principals to ask questions about seemingly innocent and accepted past practices.

The role of the school leader has changed. Rather than serving as a facility manager, today's school leader is expected to weave together the wants, needs, and demands of stakeholders into a coherent school program that meets the needs of all students. A significant part of this new responsibility requires an understanding, appreciation, and application of legal and ethical principles to school leadership (Stader, 2007, p. 1).

Diana Ellis is a beginning principal of a middle school in a large metropolitan area. Orange Grove Middle School serves approximately 900 students who live in the community around the school and a nearby public housing project. The student population is ethnically diverse with 45% African American, 25% Asian, 15% Hispanic, 10% Caucasian, and 5% "Other." Socioeconomically, the school lacks diversity as 96% of the students qualify for the U.S. Department of Agriculture free or reduced-price lunch program. Most parents work in service jobs such as hotel custodians or restaurant cooks. Both education and athletics are important to this community. Although many students are from single-parent households, parents value the chance education offers their children to have a better life. Moreover, parents and students recognize that high academic achievement makes college a reality through scholarship and grant opportunities.

The former principal, Mr. Wilson, was a veteran educator with 23 years experience at Orange Grove Middle School. His decisions and actions were never questioned. Teachers and parents were comfortable that disciplinary incidents were handled efficiently and fairly. Mr. Wilson was regarded as a strong authority figure who knew students by name and allowed teachers independence to teach as they wanted to with little or no direction from him. The one activity Mr. Wilson was credited with organizing was a quarterly banquet for students with good behavior. He worked with the cafeteria manager to sponsor a Friday night banquet for students nominated by homeroom teachers for good behavior and their parents.

Before he retired, Mr. Wilson spent two afternoons with Diana Ellis explaining facts and figures about the school community and financial resources of the school. He developed a list of needs to be addressed. Mr. Wilson also had the secretary prepare purchase orders for materials to begin the next school year. Among the purchase orders was one made to *Central City Food Service* for a new tilt skillet for the school cafeteria. Before he left on the second afternoon, Mr. Wilson encouraged Diana Ellis to sign all cafeteria purchase orders right away so that supplies and equipment would be delivered before the first day of school and the quarterly Good Behavior Banquet. Mr. Wilson and the cafeteria manager had planned a menu of spaghetti and meatballs that would be prepared in the new tilt skillet. In this case, new principal Diana Ellis confronted the accepted practices of a former principal that could be viewed to be in conflict with state regulations and the state ethics code for educators.

FACTORS TO CONSIDER

- Adherence to laws, regulations, and policies related to school accounting procedures
- Collaboration with personnel regarding school-sponsored rewards for students
- Ethical decision making
- Administrative responsibilities/accountability for school funds

THE CASE

One of the first objectives Diana Ellis had when she moved into the principal's office at Orange Grove Middle School was to meet the faculty and staff. After the first official faculty meeting, she devoted time to talking to each teacher, aide, custodian, and cafeteria worker on an individual basis during the days before students arrived and classes began. She expected resistance to the change in principals. Because Mr. Wilson had been principal for 23 years, she expected teachers to challenge her authority and to question her approaches to instructional leadership. Diana was surprised to find faculty and staff friendly and accepting of the change in leadership. One of the teachers commented to her that it was "nice to have a principal who values instruction, something more than just maintaining order."

Because her focus was on instruction, Diana spent much of the first month of school visiting classrooms, making schedule adjustments and changes, and talking to school personnel about their needs and vision for the year ahead. It was two months before the first Good Behavior Banquet when the cafeteria manager approached her to ask about the new tilt skillet. She explained that she had given Mr. Wilson a list of specifications for the skillet last May. After the cafeteria manager left, Diana found the purchase order that Mr. Wilson left in the folder on her desk. It was already made out to Central City Food Service, but Diana was unable to find notes of paperwork that reflected bids from the major suppliers of cafeteria supplies and equipment. She returned the purchase order to the folder on her desk and paged the school secretary, who also was the bookkeeper, to come to her office.

When Mrs. Bailey, the secretary/bookkeeper, reported to Diana's office, she brought a copy of the last monthly financial report for the school. The cafeteria account showed a balance of $49,717. In addition to the purchase of a tilt skillet, the cafeteria account had to maintain at least $38,000 to support two months' operating expenses. Diana was challenged to compare prices of tilt skillets that would total no more than $11,700.

Diana pulled the purchase order for the tilt skillet prepared by Mr. Wilson from the folder on her desk. The cost of the skillet from Central City Food Service was $12,075. Concerned that the bidding process hadn't been followed to support this purchase order, Diana asked the bookkeeper about the matter. The bookkeeper told her that Mr. Wilson hadn't requested bids; he always preferred to do business with Central City Food Service. The secretary's comment explained the contents of an envelope Diana found in the top drawer of the desk in her office. It contained a $150 gift certificate to an expensive restaurant in the business district of the city. The gift certificate was in a business envelope from Central City Food Service. A sticky note that read "Personal Property of John Wilson" was attached to the front of the open envelope.

Diana knew that state law required adherence to bids laws whenever purchases greater than $7,500 were necessary. The bid process mandated development of specifications for the purchase, advertisement of the bid, and acceptance of at least three sealed bids opened in public as stipulated in the bid notice. Moreover, the State Code of Ethics for Educators prohibited principals from *soliciting* gifts or favors from vendors for "things of value." A veteran principal told her that it was an accepted practice for principals to accept gifts of less than $300 from vendors. As long as the principals couldn't be viewed as soliciting the gifts, they couldn't be accused of violating the ethics code.

Diana located the specifications form for the tilt skillet that the cafeteria manager had prepared the previous spring and submitted the advertisement for the item to the school district business office. On Thursday of the week that bids for the tilt skillet were solicited on Monday, a representative from Central City Food Service made a visit to the school. Diana missed his visit because she was in a classroom. However, when she returned to her office, she found an envelope on her desk with the note, "Enjoy a night out and dinner with your husband! I appreciate your business and hope to continue an established relationship with Orange Grove Middle School. Compliments of Central City Food Service." The envelope contained a gift certificate for $100 to Angus, the most expensive steakhouse in town, and two tickets to a jazz concert valued at $60.

Once all bids for the tilt skillet were received and opened in public, it was learned that one vendor submitted a bid lower than the Central City Food Service bid. Packer Foods Company submitted a bid of $11,500, a bid $575 less than the Central City Food Service one. Although the Packer Foods Company bid for the tilt skillet was less than the Central City Food Service bid, the Central City bid included a note that a five-year warranty would be included with the purchase. The Packer Foods Company bid included a three-year warranty. The assistant superintendent for business services turned to Diana. "Which vendor do you want to choose, Mrs. Ellis? Do you want to pay the lesser amount for the skillet with a three-year warranty? Or do you want to pay the higher amount justified by the five-year warranty?"

Questions

1. What components of existing law and the State Code of Ethics for Educators make this decision difficult?

2. Which vendor, Central City Food Service or Packer Food Company, do you think Diana should select?

3. Do you think Diana should keep the gift certificate to the Angus Steakhouse? Why or why not?

4. Should Diana speak to the superintendent about the envelope containing the gift certificate to Mr. Wilson that she found in her desk?

5. Should Diana clarify the bid process with the school secretary and cafeteria manager? Why or why not?

Activities

1. Role-play a conference with the cafeteria manager and bookkeeper about the bid process and procedures to be used for purchase of the tilt skillet.

2. Draft a memo to the assistant superintendent of business services requesting approval to secure bids for the tilt skillet.

3. Discuss the ethics of the "fine line" between accepting gifts that are unsolicited as opposed to actively soliciting gifts.

4. Identify staff and community leaders important to the budget process and financial procedures of a school.

5. Debate these conflicting statements:
   - Principals should be allowed to accept gifts of $250 or less from vendors.
   - Principals should not be allowed to accept gifts of any value from vendors.

ISLLC Standards

STANDARD 3—A school administrator is an educational leader who promotes the success of all students by ensuring management of the organization, operations, and resources for a safe, efficient, and effective learning environment.

Knowledge

The administrator has knowledge and understanding of:

- Principles and issues relating to fiscal operations of school management
- Legal issues impacting school operations

Dispositions

The administrator believes in, values, and is committed to:

- Accepting responsibility
- High-quality standards, expectations, and performances
- Involving stakeholders in management processes

Performances

The administrator facilitates processes and engages in activities ensuring that:

- Potential problems and opportunities are identified
- Fiscal resources of the school are managed responsibly, efficiently, and effectively

---

STANDARD 5—A school administrator is an educational leader who promotes the success of all students by acting with integrity, fairness, and in an ethical manner.

Knowledge

The administrator has knowledge and understanding of:

- Various ethical frameworks and perspectives on ethics
- Professional codes of ethics

Dispositions

The administrator believes in, values, and is committed to:

- Bringing ethical principles to the decision-making process
- Accepting the consequences for upholding one's principles and actions

Performances

The administrator:

- Examines personal and professional values
- Demonstrates a personal and professional code of ethics
- Serves as a role model

REFERENCE

Stader, D. L. (2007). *Law and ethics in educational leadership*. Upper Saddle River, NJ: Pearson Education.

CASE 17

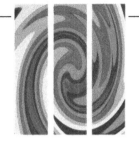

Unprofessional Behavior

A Teacher Retains a Student Who Didn't Fail

The decision to promote or retain students is one of the most difficult that an administrator makes. A student's failure in a course in high school means a deficiency in the number of Carnegie Units required for graduation. Retention in elementary school is different but has serious long-term implications.

Students fail for a variety of reasons. Some are unable to demonstrate minimum competencies expected by their teacher. Others develop poor attendance habits and are indifferent to the opportunities that school offers them. School district attendance officers are overwhelmed by referrals of students with excessive absences and have time to investigate only the most serious cases.

The No Child Left Behind Act (NCLB) does not prohibit retaining students. Those decisions are the prerogative of local boards of education, but the question that principals and teachers must answer is whether or not children can fail. If the school's philosophy is that they cannot, then one dilemma is resolved. If retention is an option, the task is to develop a fair, systematic procedure based on academic standards and communicate requirements to students, parents, and teachers.

NCLB requires that all students master core subject matter content over time. High-stakes testing and a federal mandate that students must be taught by Highly Qualified teachers means that principals must hire the best faculty and offer them professional development opportunities to ensure that they are helping their students to succeed.

Extensive research about retention is available to school administrators who are considering this matter. Wiles and Bondi (1996) offer a cogent synopsis of the literature: "Recent research on retention continues to show its inappropriateness as a means of adjusting for individual differences" (p. 3).

Retention continues to be a popular policy in most schools, according to Ubben and Hughes (1997), who warn that "it does not work as a method of maintaining standards; it does not work as a means of threatening children to perform" (p. 183). Teachers and principals might argue that failure is the natural consequence of poor performance or indifference to school attendance requirements, and there are no other options available for a student who has not met school standards.

There are few tasks more daunting than informing a high school student of credit withheld for course failure or telling the parents of a fourth grader that their child has failed. It is better, as Ubben and Hughes suggest, "to use instructional process solutions to adjust for individual differences along the way" (p. 184).

Finding solutions means that principals and teachers must identify at-risk students *early* in the semester and create learning strategies that address their learning deficiencies. Tutoring and individual remediation are conventional methods, and parent involvement and support are especially important.

If the faculty agree that retaining students for academic deficiencies, poor attendance, or other reasons is congruent with their core beliefs about learning and children, a procedure should be developed that includes

1. Identifying students who are having learning problems early in the semester or year.

2. Retaining work samples from at-risk students that illustrate the difficulties they're having. Teachers should also keep examples of acceptable work to avoid accusations of bias.

3. Meeting with parents early to advise them about their child's progress and to encourage their participation in getting help.

4. Sending written notice to parents advising them that their child may fail a course or is at risk of retention. Teachers should keep a copy of warning letters.

5. Meeting at midterm in high school or in the spring in elementary school with an administrator and other faculty who teach the at-risk student. The student's grades, attendance, attitude, and other factors that influence achievement should be discussed. This conference is the appropriate forum in which work samples and information pertaining to parental notification should be discussed.

6. Making a decision about the student's placement or credit. Consensus is important. This meeting is the place to talk about changes to the student's instructional environment. It is the school's responsibility to alter variables it controls that contributed to failure.

7. Explaining the school's decision to parents and the student. They have a right to appeal the decision to the board of education.

8. Following up during the next term to see if the student is successful in the course the second time. Data gathered over several years can show whether either withholding credit or retaining students had the intended effect. Administrators should share this information with faculty annually since student retention will always be a controversial topic.

FACTORS TO CONSIDER

- Benefits of retaining students or withholding credit
- Teacher attitudes about retention
- Social promotion
- Academic standards for special education students
- Board of education policies about retaining students or withholding credit

THE CASE

Tom Masters walked briskly through the hallways of Stafford Elementary School. He wanted to visit as many of the 18 classrooms in his building as he could on this last day of school, and the kids would be leaving for summer vacation in a few minutes.

He turned the corner to the fourth grade hall and saw David Fisher standing in the doorway to Mrs. Denny's room, waiting for the bell that would release him to weeks of swimming, baseball games, and no school. David had attended Stafford since kindergarten and came from a home in which both parents worked at menial jobs to make ends meet. David's older brother, Jacob, was in the sixth grade.

Tom smiled as he approached David. "Ready for the summer?"

"Yeah! I'm tired of school!"

Tom nodded. "To tell you the truth, I'm ready for a break, too."

"I don't think my parents are going to be too happy with my grades," David frowned.

Tom noticed that David was holding his report card by his side.

"Oh? How'd you do?"

David shrugged and gave the document to Tom. "Not so hot."

Tom scanned the report. David had earned five "C's," a "D" in math, and failed reading. It was obvious that the reading grade had been changed from "D" to "F." Mrs. Denny had written a notice on the back of the report card to David's parents telling them that he'd have to repeat the fourth grade, which was consistent with the school's policy for a student who failed either reading or math.

Tom paused. He'd heard of students changing report card grades upward, but never in the opposite direction.

"Looks like your reading grade was changed," Tom said. "Did you do that?"

David shrugged and shook his head. "Mrs. Denny did."

"Why?"

David shrugged his shoulders again. "Don't know."

The bell rang and Mrs. Denny appeared at the door to lead her students to their buses.

"Mrs. Denny," Tom said, "I noticed that David's reading grade was changed to an 'F'".

Did you make a mistake when you put it on the report card?"

"No," the teacher replied. "He earned a low 'D.'"

Tom was incredulous. "We'd better talk about this. Come to my office as soon as your kids are on the buses."

Masters said good-bye to students as they hurried through the hallways, but returned to his office several minutes ahead of Mrs. Denny. She knocked softly on his door.

"You said you wanted to see me?" she asked, standing in the doorway.

"Yes. Come in, please," Tom said, pointing to a chair.

"I looked at David's report card," he began, "and the changed grade was obvious. I'm sure his parents would have noticed. I've never known a student to *lower* a grade, though. When I asked, David said you'd made the change, but you told me that you hadn't made an error. I don't understand."

"Do you remember when you met with the fourth grade teachers to talk about students who might have to be retained next year?"

"Sure," Masters replied, "and, as I recall, you didn't recommend any of your kids."

"Well," Mrs. Denny began, "you asked me after the meeting if I understood the school's procedure for retention since I've never suggested that anyone should fail."

"I remember," Tom nodded. "I just wanted to make sure that you understood. You've only been here for three years."

The teacher nodded. "I thought you were trying to tell me that someone had to fail. David was my weakest student in reading and another year in fourth grade wouldn't hurt him."

The principal was amazed. The school's promotion procedures had been designed to help resolve the problems associated with social promotion and to establish reasonable standards for student performance. He reviewed them early in the year with faculty to make sure they understood what they were doing.

"Let me make sure I understand," he said in disbelief. "You're telling me that David was retained because you *thought* you were required to fail someone? Did you believe you had a retention quota?"

"Well, no," the teacher replied, shifting uncomfortably in the chair, "but you seemed concerned that I hadn't retained anyone since I've been here."

Tom paused. Mrs. Denny's judgment had created a serious problem, and he had to decide what to do now.

Questions

1. What steps should Tom take to correct Mrs. Denny's error?

2. What should Tom say to Mrs. Denny?

3. Should Mrs. Denny receive a formal reprimand for her decision? Why or why not?

Activities

1. Role-play the rest of the conference between Mr. Masters and Mrs. Denny.

2. Interview your principal and talk about the positive and negative elements associated with failing students.

3. Would you consider placing a letter of reprimand in Mrs. Denny's personnel file because of her arbitrary decision to change David's reading grade? If so, write the letter and share its contents with your class.

4. Find two journal articles about retention and share them with your class. Did you discover a consistent theme in the articles? If so, what was it?

5. Interview your school's administrator to learn how he or she feels about retention. What standards are used to help make decisions about promoting or retaining students? What efforts are made to change the conditions under which a student has failed (i.e., the teacher or subject matter)?

ISLLC Standards

STANDARD 1—A school administrator is an educational leader who promotes the success of all students by facilitating the development, articulation, implementation, and stewardship of a vision of learning that is shared and supported by the school community.

Knowledge

The administrator has knowledge and understanding of:

- Systems theory
- Effective consensus-building and negotiation skills

Dispositions

The administrator believes in, values, and is committed to:

- A school vision of high standards of learning
- A willingness to continuously examine one's own assumptions, beliefs, and practices

Performances

The administrator facilitates processes and engages in activities ensuring that:

- The vision shapes the educational programs, plans, and activities
- Assessment data related to student learning are used to develop the school vision and goals

---

STANDARD 2—A school administrator is an educational leader who promotes the success of all students by advocating, nurturing, and sustaining a school culture and instructional program conducive to student learning and professional growth.

Knowledge

The administrator has knowledge and understanding of:

- Applied motivational theories
- Curriculum design, implementation, evaluation, and refinement

Dispositions

The administrator believes in, values, and is committed to:

- A safe and supportive learning environment
- Preparing students to be contributing members of society

Performances

The administrator facilitates processes and engages in activities ensuring that:

- Students and staff feel valued and important
- Multiple sources of information regarding performances are used by staff and students

REFERENCE

Ubben, G. C., & Hughes, L. W. (1997). *The principal: Creative leadership for effective schools*. Boston: Allyn & Bacon.

CASE 18

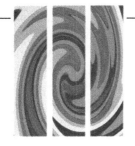

It All Depends on the Numbers

Teacher Success Is Based on Test Scores

The No Child Left Behind Act (NCLB) was signed into law on January 8, 2002. Major components of the law include accountability for student achievement of academic standards, increased flexibility and local control, a greater role for parents in their children's education programs, and greater emphasis on the use of scientifically based instruction. More specifically, aspects of this legislation require setting higher educational standards and testing of students in Grades 3 through 8 on an annual basis. States are required to report assessment results to school districts prior to the beginning of the school year in a disaggregated format for analysis by gender, ethnicity, poverty levels, disability, migrant status, and limited English proficiency. Principals must ensure that 95% of students in all subgroups are in attendance on days when state and national assessments are administered.

Once annual test results are analyzed, schools are either rewarded for meeting Adequate Yearly Progress (AYP) goals or they face sanctions for failing to do so. Schools that reflect progress in all but one area, such as special education, are categorized as schools in need of improvement. When schools fail to achieve AYP for two years, parents must be afforded the opportunity to transfer their children to another school that has demonstrated success in meeting AYP goals. Schools failing to achieve AYP for two consecutive years and categorized as schools in need of improvement are in jeopardy of "reconstitution," which basically means that the principal will be reassigned or dismissed and that teachers will be transferred to other schools while selected teachers will be reassigned to the school.

Other provisions of the NCLB require states to guarantee that teachers are highly qualified and that paraprofessionals either hold an associate's degree or demonstrate that they possess skills to support quality school improvement as measured by a state or locally developed assessment. The NCLB also requires that staff development activities provided for professional and support employees be based on scientific research. Staff development must have a sustained impact on effective classroom instruction, enhance the use of technology, and relate to school and district improvement plans.

The NCLB includes provisions that address a quality instructional program without mandating use of specific materials or commercial programs. Reading is identified as key to success for students in the early grades. Teachers and principals are required to employ techniques for teaching reading that include systematic instruction in decoding, fluency, and comprehension. At the secondary level, high schools are required to increase participation in Advanced Placement programs among low-income students. Provisions of the NCLB also require schools to establish safe environments for students and to make data related to school safety and drug use available to the public.

These principles guarantee that all students have opportunities to develop their full potential. While the principles of this federal legislation read well and express a commitment to providing quality educational programs for all students, the impact of the NCLB has altered the landscape of public education in ways not considered by its authors. Since passage of this legislation, professional journals have contained articles with titles such as "No Child Left Behind: Promise or Rhetoric?" (Rose, 2003) and "When Raising Isn't Rising" (Wolf, 2002). In this case, a principal recognized by her peers as a highly effective principal is challenged by requirements of the NCLB.

FACTORS TO CONSIDER

- Administrator and teacher responsibilities for compliance with provisions of the NCLB
- Staff development for professional and support personnel to address requirements of the NCLB
- Faculty and staff planning and collaboration in response to change
- Use of data to drive the instructional program of a school and school district

Elaine Lewis is a veteran principal of Newcomb Elementary School, a K–5 school with the reputation of being the "top" school in the Central City Public Schools District. She is one of eight elementary principals in the district. Elaine's school has a student population that reflects the diversity of Central City. Of the approximately 770 students at Newcomb Elementary School, 40% are white, 35% are African American, 15% are Hispanic, 5% are Asian, and 5% are classified as "Other." Despite past tensions among the different groups, Elaine has worked with her PTA and community leaders to establish harmony among all groups and to demonstrate respect for all people. The faculty at Newcomb Elementary School parallels the diversity of the student population.

Of the 42 teachers assigned to Newcomb, approximately 45% are white, 38% are African American, 15% are Hispanic, and 2% are Asian.

When components of the NCLB were first presented to principals in Central City Public Schools, Elaine embraced the goal of improving student achievement and establishing rigorous courses of study. She studied provisions of the law and volunteered to serve on a district committee to develop an administrative infrastructure to address compliance with components of the NCLB. Elaine enthusiastically introduced changes brought about by provisions of the NCLB. She emphasized the benefits of routine monitoring of student progress and use of state tests to measure student achievement to teachers and parents. Elaine highlighted the positive features of the NCLB and assured teachers that they would work together to meet the challenges imposed by this legislation; she expressed confidence in her staff that achieving annual goals would easily be within their grasp. Elaine supported her charge to teachers with the words of DuFour, DuFour, Eaker, and Karhanek (2004):

> Teachers were more likely to acknowledge the need for improvement when they jointly studied evidence of the strengths and weaknesses of their school. They were more likely to arrive at consensus on the most essential knowledge and skills students should acquire when together they analyzed and discussed state and national standards, district curriculum guides, and student achievement data. They were more likely to agree on the most effective instructional strategies when they worked together in examining results from their common assessments. (p. 137)

Elaine formed a committee of teacher volunteers to suggest ways for the school faculty and staff to successfully implement requirements of the NCLB. The committee developed a list of varied instructional methods and techniques that teachers and special area staff such as the library/media specialist, the counselor, and special education teachers could use to strengthen the instructional program. The committee also developed a model of collaborative teaching that established teams of teachers to address the individual needs of children identified as low-performing students. The superintendent of Central City Public Schools, Dr. Ron Taylor, was so impressed with Newcomb Elementary School's approach to implementing NCLB requirements that he encouraged principals and teachers from the other elementary schools to visit Newcomb and to collaborate with Newcomb teachers.

So far, so good. Test scores at the end of the first year of the NCLB were strong for Newcomb students. At the end of the second year governed by the NCLB, Newcomb test scores neither increased nor decreased. Students maintained the previous year's test score levels. During the third year of the NCLB implementation, a new subdivision was opened in the attendance area for Newcomb Elementary School. More than 700 residential units were constructed, sold, and occupied by single-family households within 11 months. This population increase was due to expansion of a local manufacturing business. Increased job opportunities in the area resulted in a stronger local economy and a growing population. Newcomb experienced an increase in student population of 155 students.

Elaine met with the NCLB lead committee of teachers to discuss how best to accommodate population growth, especially in special education, at Newcomb. She said to these lead teachers, "I'm concerned about the impact this sudden population increase will have on our ability to achieve AYP for this year. While I know how hard teachers work and collaborate to address the needs of all students, the general public looks only at test scores reported in the paper. Time to address the needs of our new students, particularly those identified to receive special education services, is short. What ideas for meeting this challenge do you have?"

Mrs. Peterson, a fourth grade teacher, spoke up first. "I'm tired of being judged by test scores of students. The state tests that we are required to use force us to structure daily lessons in a drill and practice format. We don't have the leeway to be creative with our teaching anymore. I don't remember when I truly enjoyed a full day of teaching. Requirements of NCLB have taken the fun out of teaching!"

Comments by several other teachers echoed Mrs. Peterson's sentiments. Elaine was shocked and dismayed. She had begun to sense that teachers were stressed because of pressures to achieve AYP, but she hadn't realized that teachers' frustrations were so strong. For the next hour, Elaine sat back and listened as teachers voiced concerns about teaching to the test, lack of time to integrate art and music with subjects such as social studies and science, and fatigue from frequently being observed by teachers from other schools.

For several days, Elaine thoughtfully considered remarks made by teachers on the NCLB lead committee. She was perplexed by the stress evidenced by teachers' remarks during the hour-long meeting. She had been so sure that enthusiasm and confidence in her teachers would minimize the increased pressure of accountability imposed by the NCLB. Elaine wasn't sure how to address the stress the teachers were feeling, but she realized that she needed help from outside the school to identify ways to support her teachers. It was 4 P.M. She knew that this was the best time to reach Ed Thompson, assistant superintendent of curriculum and instruction for Central City Public Schools.

Elaine was in luck. Dr. Thompson was available to talk with her. In fact, when he answered the telephone, he said, "I'm glad you've called. I need to talk with you."

"Sure," responded Elaine, "I need to talk with you, too. I need your help. The increase in student population at Newcomb has added additional pressure to the stress teachers are feeling to maintain our success achieving AYP."

"I'll be happy to work with you and teachers at Newcomb to address your concerns, Elaine, but the reason I need to talk with you is more pressing," said Dr. Thompson.

"I don't understand," countered Elaine. "What's going on?"

"Well," Dr. Thompson began, "You know how adamant the school board is about ethical administration of standardized tests. The policy passed just last year includes a statement that addresses required procedures of test administration and prohibits prompting of items on all commercial, locally produced, and standardized tests. It seems that one of the visiting teachers who observed a third grade teacher administering a state test claims that the Newcomb teacher violated test administration procedures. The visiting teacher told her principal that she observed the Newcomb teacher prompting students with tips for answering certain test items. She said that as the teacher monitored students' work, she paused at desks and nodded yes or no as students marked selected test items. Your teachers are more stressed about achieving AYP than we've realized!"

Questions

1. How should Elaine react to accusations made by the visiting teacher?

2. How can Elaine determine the truth of the visiting teacher's accusations?

3. If the accusations are false, how should Elaine respond? If the accusations are true, what should Elaine do?

4. What measures should Elaine employ to address concerns expressed by Newcomb teachers?

5. Discuss Elaine's approach to meeting requirements of the NCLB. What other measures should she have considered?

Activities

1. Outline a response to the NCLB committee of teachers regarding their concerns.

2. Role-play a conference with the teacher accused of violating test administration procedures.

3. Discuss ways for the Newcomb faculty to address the sudden increase in student population.

4. Draft a letter to the superintendent requesting that visits by other schools be rescheduled "until further notice."

5. Develop a PowerPoint presentation to acquaint new principals and teachers with provisions of the NCLB.

ISLLC Standards

STANDARD 5—A school administrator is an educational leader who promotes the success of all students by acting with integrity, fairness, and in an ethical manner.

Knowledge

The administrator has knowledge and understanding of:
- The purpose of education and the role of leadership in modern society
- Professional codes of ethics

Dispositions

The administrator believes in, values, and is committed to:
- Bringing ethical principles to the decision-making process
- Using the influence of one's office constructively and productively in the service of all students and their families

Performances

The administrator:
- Demonstrates values, beliefs, and attitudes that inspire others to higher levels of performance

- Expects that others in the school community will demonstrate integrity and exercise ethical behavior

---

STANDARD 6—A school administrator is an educational leader who promotes the success of all students by understanding, responding to, and influencing the larger political, social, economic, legal, and cultural context.

Knowledge

The administrator has knowledge and understanding of:

- The political, social, cultural, and economic systems and processes that impact schools
- Models and strategies of change and conflict resolution as applied to the larger political, social, cultural, and economic contexts of schooling

Dispositions

The administrator believes in, values, and is committed to:

- The importance of a continuing dialogue with other decision makers affecting education
- Active participation in the political and policy-making context in the service of education

Performances

The administrator facilitates processes and engages in activities ensuring that:

- Communication occurs among the school community concerning trends, issues, and potential changes in the environment in which schools operate
- The school community works within the framework of policies, laws, and regulations enacted by local, state, and federal authorities

REFERENCES

DuFour, R., DuFour, R., Eaker, R., & Karhanek, G. (2004). *Whatever it takes.* Bloomington, IN: National Educational Service.

Rose, L. C. (2003). No child left behind: Promise or rhetoric? *Phi Delta Kappan, 84*(5), 338.

Wolf, D. P. (2002). When raising isn't rising. *The School Administrator, 59,* 20–23.

CASE 19

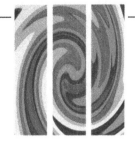

All A's Are Not Enough

Rewards Must Be Earned

One of the most prestigious honors a high school student can receive is selection for membership in the National Honor Society (NHS). The NHS is recognized as one of the nation's finest organizations established to recognize outstanding high school students. Students in Grades 10 through 12 are nominated for membership by teachers each year. To be eligible for membership, students must demonstrate excellence in the areas of scholarship, leadership, service, character, and citizenship. Students selected, or "tapped," for membership in the NHS participate in service projects in their community, such as tutoring other students.

Most high schools designate a special day and time to schedule an annual NHS induction. Students elected to leadership positions lead a special ceremony that describes the purposes of the NHS and features qualities that students must demonstrate in order to be eligible for membership. These ceremonies typically are solemn occasions open to all students and parents.

Prior to the induction ceremony, a committee of teachers confers to identify new students eligible for membership. This committee reviews application forms, recommendations from teachers, students' grades, and an account of student participation in extracurricular and service activities. Research by Gordon, Bridglall, and Meroe (2004) supports the conclusion that "high academic achievement is closely associated with exposure to family and community-based activities and learning experiences that occur both in and out of school in support of academic learning." Only students with grade point averages of

2.75 and above on a four-point scale are considered eligible for membership. From among students with averages that meet this criterion, the committee evaluates teacher recommendations and students' participation in school and community activities. Parents and students may mistakenly think that membership in the NHS is based strictly on academic standing or scholarship, but students also must demonstrate qualities of leadership, service, character, and citizenship. The NHS is more than just an honor roll. NHS chapters establish rules for membership that are based on a student's outstanding performance in the areas of scholarship, service, leadership, and character. These four criteria for selection form the foundation on which the organization and its activities are built.

Membership in the NHS is valued at Excel High School. Students compete for high grades and consider a position on the school's High Academic Team to be one of prestige. Excel High School is located in a rural area, home to many families that earn their living from farming and forestry. The largest senior class recorded in the school's history numbered only 79. This year's senior class has 66 students. Consequently, students know one another and their families well.

Because Excel High School is comparatively small with fewer teachers than many schools in metropolitan areas, extracurricular activities for students are limited. Students may participate in athletics including football, basketball, and track, or they can choose to focus on music and be a member of the high school marching band. The only other activities available for high school students are membership in the Key Club, the Interact Club, or the senior class play. Since there are limited opportunities for recognition among their fellow students, membership in the NHS becomes all the more important.

Principal Don Adams appointed Tina Scott, the Spanish teacher, sponsor of the NHS three years ago. Since Señora Scott assumed responsibility for its members and their activities, the NHS at Excel High School has been very active—delivering meals to senior citizens on weekends and holidays and supporting the fundraising efforts of the local heart association chapter, for example. Mr. Adams has received several letters from parents complimenting Señora Scott's faculty leadership of this group. Fellow teachers have remarked that she has affirmed the importance of membership among students at all grade levels. Señora Scott is credited with changing the image of NHS members from one of "geeks" to one of "cool dudes." Students want to be identified with the NHS, whereas in past years, membership was considered the mark of an unpopular student.

When the time of the year arrived for NHS nominations, Señora Scott distributed nomination forms to teachers at a faculty meeting. Teachers had two weeks to nominate eligible students and return the forms to her. Twenty-eight nominations were submitted. The NHS teacher review committee met one afternoon after school. After reviewing and discussing all nominations, they found that 21 students met academic requirements for membership. The teacher review committee met another afternoon during the same week to discuss the leadership, character, service, and citizenship qualities of the 21 students. The quality of citizenship attributed to one female student was discussed extensively. Although the student met academic requirements (in fact, her transcript reflected all A's), the teachers recounted several incidents in which the student was disrespectful to other students and to adults. One teacher commented that the student's parents called her one evening and complained because the student told them she was singled out in class for misbehaving. The student's description of the incident was exaggerated, creating tension between the parents and teacher. After discussion and consideration of this student's poor display of character and citizenship, the teachers disapproved her nomination for membership in the NHS.

FACTORS TO CONSIDER

- School and community relationships
- Recognition of student achievement
- Student participation in extracurricular activities
- Criteria for recognizing student achievement

THE CASE

The day before the NHS tapping ceremony, Señora Scott asked Mr. Adams if she could speak with him for a minute. Mr. Adams nodded "yes" and extended his arm for her to move into his office before him.

"Please sit down, Señora," Mr. Adams motioned for her to sit in one of the two upholstered chairs in his office. As he sat in the other chair, which was on the same side of his desk as Señora, he asked, "What can I do for you?"

"I feel as though I need to make you aware of the discussion during the NHS teacher review committee. Of the 21 academically eligible students, one student, Lauren Mills, was disapproved by all teachers on the committee. Although Lauren is a bright student, she has been unpleasant with teachers and other students. The teachers don't feel that she reflects qualities of a good citizen. They feel that Lauren's attitude displays poor character."

"Well, you know that I trust the judgment of teachers on this committee, Señora. If they feel the student doesn't uphold NHS standards, then she shouldn't be selected for membership," he responded.

Señora Scott looked thoughtful as she said, "I appreciate your support and confidence, Mr. Adams. I just felt you should be made aware of this situation in case the parents are upset. They have given one of the other teachers a hard time."

"Thanks, Señora. I'll be prepared in case the parents have questions."

The induction ceremony began at 9:00 A.M. the following morning. Students from ninth through twelfth grade sat on one side of the gym, while parents and guests sat on the other side. Officers and current members of the NHS were seated on the gym floor in position to host the induction ceremony. The officers took turns explaining the purpose of the NHS and describing the qualities of its members. At a signal from the president, current NHS members moved among the students seated in the bleachers and tapped those selected for membership this year.

Once all new members had moved to the gym floor, a loud voice called out, "I don't believe this!"

Mr. Adams turned to see the parents of the "all-A" student whom the faculty didn't approve for NHS membership step down from the bleachers and out the door of the gym. Officers of the NHS finished the induction ceremony and thanked parents and guests for taking time to attend.

At 3:30 P.M. and after all buses and most students had cleared the school parking lot, Mr. Adams returned to his office. Just as he sat down, he heard an angry voice in front of the school. He looked out the window and saw Lauren Mills's mother angrily speaking to Señora Scott as Señora was walking to her car. Mr. Adams left his office and walked to the parking lot. He told Señora Scott to go and pick up her child at daycare and that he would address the parent's concerns. Then he asked Mrs. Mills if she would like to come with him to his office.

Once in the office, Mrs. Mills continued her tirade. She accused Señora and the other teachers of mistreating her daughter. Mrs. Mills claimed that her daughter Lauren was devastated, that she would suffer irreparable emotional harm because she wasn't selected for membership in the NHS. "What are you going to do about this?" she demanded of Mr. Adams.

Mr. Adams answered, "I regret that Lauren and you are disappointed, Mrs. Mills. Yes, Lauren has made all A's her freshman and sophomore years in high school, but membership in the NHS requires more than just high academic standing. As you heard the NHS officers explain this morning, students tapped for membership must demonstrate qualities of leadership, service, character, and citizenship in addition to scholarship.

"What are you saying? That my daughter isn't a good citizen or a capable leader? Or are you implying that her character is deficient? Lauren has certainly met requirements of service by volunteering at the assisted living facility once a week. I'll have you know that several of the other parents called me this afternoon to ask why she wasn't included among the new students. They don't understand either. My daughter is one of the best students this school has ever seen!"

"I agree that she is a smart student, but you need to talk with Lauren about her attitude toward others," Mr. Adams stated. "As I've said to you, membership in the NHS is dependent on qualities other than just high academic standing."

Mrs. Mills stood and moved toward the door of Mr. Adams's office, "I don't need to talk with my daughter, Mr. Adams. I know how polite and respectful she is to everyone. I expect a full investigation of this matter and an explanation in writing. My husband and I plan to see an attorney, and I have an appointment with the superintendent in the morning!"

Questions

1. What do you think about the way Mr. Adams handled the conference with Señora Scott when he first learned that the decision of the NHS teacher review committee had created a potential problem?

2. Should the parent have been notified prior to the NHS induction ceremony that her daughter was not going to be tapped?

3. Who needs to be involved with resolving this situation?

4. How should Mr. Adams handle the parent's announcement that she has an appointment with the superintendent in the morning?

5. How should Mr. Adams deal with the parent's threat to see an attorney?

Activities

1. Outline a plan of action for the principal to follow in response to the parent's complaint.

2. Draft a letter to the parent in response to her demand for a written explanation of reasons why her daughter wasn't selected for NHS membership.

3. Role-play a telephone conversation with the superintendent alerting him to the parent's concerns.

4. Discuss legal precedents that relate to similar situations.

5. Role-play a follow-up conference with the parent.

ISLLC Standards

STANDARD 1—A school administrator is an educational leader who promotes the success of all students by facilitating the development, articulation, implementation, and stewardship of a vision of learning that is shared and supported by the school community.

Knowledge

The administrator has knowledge and understanding of:

- Effective communication
- Effective consensus-building and negotiation skills

Dispositions

The administrator believes in, values, and is committed to:

- A school vision of high standards of learning
- Doing the work required for high levels of personal and organization performance

Performances

The administrator facilitates processes and engages in activities ensuring that:

- The vision and mission of the school are effectively communicated to staff, parents, students, and community members
- The vision and mission are communicated through the use of symbols, ceremonies, stories, and similar activities

---

STANDARD 5—A school administrator is an educational leader who promotes the success of all students by acting with integrity, fairness, and in an ethical manner.

Knowledge

The administrator has knowledge and understanding of:

- Professional codes of ethics
- The philosophy and history of education

Dispositions

The administrator believes in, values, and is committed to:

- The ideal of the common good
- Accepting the consequences for upholding one's principles and actions

Performances

The administrator:

- Recognizes and respects the legitimate authority of others
- Examines and considers the prevailing values of the diverse school community

REFERENCE

Gordon, E. W., Bridglall, B. L., & Meroe, A. S. (2004). *Supplementary education: The hidden curriculum of high academic achievement.* Lanham, MD: Rowman & Littlefield Publishers. (ERIC Document Reproduction Service No. ED489047)

CASE 20

The Community Won't Understand!

Diversity Becomes Unpopular

Prospective administrators will find that recruiting, interviewing, and hiring teachers are among the most important functions of leadership. Making choices is inherent in each of those tasks; choosing means making judgments and assigning value to multiple variables.

Interviewers bring their own perspectives to the selection process and should guard against allowing personal biases to influence their decisions. A commitment to diversity is measured through action, not rhetoric. School leaders can expect to interact with people who adopt alternative lifestyles, purportedly a minority in society, who often must contend with ostracism if they admit their differences in a culture that values sameness. As an example, the emotional toll on children who are different or whose parents are homosexual can be devastating. These students are more likely than other youth to attempt suicide, to abuse drugs or alcohol, and to experience academic problems. A principal's advocacy includes affirming the dignity of *all* children regardless of sexual identity and helps to quell their fears of rejection and harassment by their peers.

Advocacy applies to adults, too. Laws applicable to hiring practices have a long history in our nation and prohibit discriminatory personnel practices, especially in hiring new teachers. The Equal Opportunity Employment Commission, the Office of Federal Contract Compliance, and the Department of Labor have written volumes of guidelines and regulations to ensure that all qualified job applicants receive fair consideration for position vacancies, but advocacy for minorities, women, and people with alternative lifestyles who apply for instructional or staff positions may be met with resistance from faculty and the community.

A principal's recommendation to hire an applicant is powerful and should be based on congruency between elements in a job description and an applicant's qualifications. However, personnel decisions are sometimes influenced by external issues that involve a form of patronage, or favoritism. When that happens, administrators are faced with the difficult choice of adhering to ethical principles or complying with the informal but powerful substructure of the school district's organization.

Using a team of teachers to help with hiring new faculty has become an effective way for leaders to manage the process. Gorton and Schneider (1991) suggested that teams should follow a five-step process to maximize the school's chances of hiring the most effective teachers.

First, identify and define the criteria that are important in the job. The district's Position Description will include many of them, but there may be other talents that the school needs.

Second, analyze placement papers and résumés carefully. The purpose of the documents review is to screen applicants to determine which ones should be invited for a personal interview.

Next, have the team plan carefully for interviews. What are the interview's objectives? Who will ask which questions? What questions cannot be asked? What constitutes a valid response from the applicant? How will the team make its final recommendation? What questions is the applicant likely to ask? These considerations should be addressed before the first interview is scheduled.

Fourth, interview only the most promising candidates. Thorough planning and screening procedures should assist in this step. Avoid six common errors that frequently occur during interviews: (1) posing "yes" or "no" questions that require little analysis by the applicant, (2) asking unimaginative questions for which the applicant has probably already prepared an answer, (3) asking leading questions that suggest the "right" answer, (4) asking questions that reveal the questioner's attitude about the subject, (5) asking questions unrelated to the task, and (6) asking questions already answered on the candidate's application or résumé.

Finally, make the selection and inform all candidates of the result (Gorton & Schneider, 1991, p. 198). The principal should thank those not chosen for their interest in the school and tell them that someone else is being recommended for the position, but the principal should *never* discuss the team's reasons for nonselection.

- Teacher applicants with alternative lifestyles
- Teacher interview and selection processes
- Discriminatory practices in hiring
- Ethical administrative decision making

THE CASE

Brandon Talbot placed the teacher applications he had reviewed on his desk and leaned back in his chair. There were four good candidates among seven people who had applied. That's a problem, he thought, but a nice one. Interviewing was going to be a challenge, but at least he had a margin for error.

Talbot, a teacher and an assistant principal in the district for 10 years, had been selected for the principal's job at Wellborne Middle School when his predecessor, Tom Riley, became the district's director of human relations. Brandon was reassigned in October, and this was his first opportunity to add to the school's 60-member faculty. Dr. Riley had worked for seven years to build a superior academic program and an excellent professional staff, and Brandon wanted to prove to teachers and the community that he was capable of choosing the *right* applicants, too.

Mr. Talbot was reluctant to approach the superintendent with a request to add faculty after the year began, but the school's social sciences classes were overcrowded and students' academic schedules couldn't be changed midway through the semester. He'd decided to ask for the additional teacher, and, to his surprise, the superintendent had approved the request.

Brandon decided to involve his faculty in the selection process. After all, he reasoned, its members would be working closely with the new teacher. He wanted to build trust, and it was important that they help to choose a teacher with whom they believed they could work.

The faculty was receptive to the idea. Talbot selected a team that included three members of the social sciences department, a special educator, and the media center specialist. He decided to make the selection in phases. First, he spoke with Dr. Riley to obtain a list of candidates qualified for the position. Second, he spent several hours poring over their personnel files and making notes. Satisfied that he had found the best people available, he returned to school and called the interview team to his office after school to coordinate its efforts.

"Dr. Riley said that it's important for us to have a structured interview with each applicant," he explained. "That means we have to ask the same basic set of questions to everyone. We're free, of course, to ask follow-up questions based on the responses we hear, but the interviewees should have an equal chance to respond to similar questions so that we can evaluate their responses."

Team members talked about assigning a mentor to the new teacher. They also discussed the school's need for a drama coach since Mrs. Wells, the school's longtime Drama Club sponsor, would begin maternity leave soon. Talbot explained that the team's role was to help him select the best teacher for the job, but the recommendation for employment was his alone. The team closed its meeting by assigning questions to each member about discipline, curriculum, community relations, and technology. Mrs. Winsett, the Media Center specialist, offered to make a scoring rubric to evaluate the candidates' answers.

Mr. Talbot was satisfied that his teachers were ready but worried about choosing the best person for the job, someone who would quickly become a contributor to the faculty team. Applicants were interviewed after school on two different days. Talbot allotted approximately one hour for each session. Two applicants with extensive experience in teaching social sciences in middle school quickly emerged as the most promising.

Talbot called their references, talked with administrators at schools where both applicants had taught, reevaluated transcripts and their applications, and talked with Dr. Riley about his assessments.

Dr. Martha Jeffers, with 10 years of teaching experience, appeared to be the person best suited for the position at Wellborne. Her credentials were impeccable, and she had received glowing evaluations from former administrators. Of the finalists, she alone had experience coaching a drama club.

Despite the information he had gathered, Mr. Talbot felt uneasy. If Dr. Jeffers was as good as her application indicated, why wasn't she teaching now? Someone with her talent shouldn't be available after the school year began. The team had agreed that her background and experience were impressive, but its members had been distant during her structured interview. Enthusiastic when questioning Sandra McDonald, the other candidate, teachers had asked Dr. Jeffers few follow-up questions.

The principal convened a team meeting after school on Thursday to hear its recommendation. He listened intently while members discussed their ratings and shared opinions about the interviews.

"I guess it's time for a decision," he said after 30 minutes. "I'd like to hear your final thoughts on our candidates, and perhaps we can decide which person to eliminate."

The team tallied its scores again. Talbot was surprised when Ms. McDonald, who had less teaching experience than Dr. Jeffers and no background in coaching drama, earned the highest mark.

After more discussion, Talbot closed the meeting.

"I've listened carefully to your ideas and I think all of them are important, but I'm confused about your choice of Ms. McDonald over Dr. Jeffers. We have a chance to add someone to the faculty who has a proven record of success with middle school kids, and she can coach the Drama Club, too. I'm sure Ms. McDonald will become an excellent teacher over time, but . . ."

Joan Martin, the special education representative on the team, placed her hand on Talbot's arm.

"Ms. Martin?" he said.

"Could I speak with you in the hall for just a moment?" she asked.

Talbot looked at the rest of the team. No one looked surprised.

"Certainly," he replied, standing.

"Mr. Talbot," Ms. Martin began after they'd reached the hallway and closed the conference room door behind them, "you're right about Dr. Jeffers. She *is* the best applicant we interviewed, but . . ." she said hesitantly.

"What is it, Joan? If everyone agrees that she's the best candidate, why are we hesitating?"

"I can't prove this," Ms. Martin replied, "but she has a reputation as being a lesbian."

"Why should that matter, Joan? Has she ever done anything inappropriate with students? If she has, I couldn't find evidence of it," Talbot replied.

"I don't know that she ever approached a student," Ms. Martin said, "but think about it.

"You're new and the first teacher you want to hire is a lesbian. What will happen if the rumors are true? You know parents are going to hear them, and the community won't understand!"

Talbot hesitated. Wellborne was known for its community relationships and involved parents. Many of them were civic leaders and influential in local politics.

"I'm only suggesting that you reconsider, Mr. Talbot," Ms. Martin said. "We'll support the applicant you believe will be best for the school. We wanted you to have all the information possible before making a decision."

Mr. Talbot and Ms. Martin returned to the meeting.

"Let me think about our candidates a little longer," he told the team. "I'd like to recommend someone to the superintendent by Tuesday, so let's meet again on Monday after school and I'll tell you who it's going to be."

He thanked the teachers for their hard work and walked toward his office, knowing that he faced a difficult choice over the weekend.

Questions

1. What are the ethical issues that Mr. Talbot must consider as he makes a decision?

2. Should the interview team have made Mr. Talbot aware of gossip about Dr. Jeffers? Why or why not?

3. How would your community and faculty react if a gay or lesbian teacher was hired at your school?

4. Should Mr. Talbot hire Dr. Jeffers? Why or why not?

Activities

1. Make a list of pros and cons that Mr. Talbot should consider when making his decision. Discuss your list with your colleagues.

2. Although the law is clear about discrimination in hiring, discuss the consequences of hiring a gay or lesbian teacher at your school from both a faculty and a community perspective.

3. Identify legal issues related to the confidentiality of oral and written recommendations from former employers. Discuss them with the class.

4. Role-play Mr. Talbot's meeting with the interview team on Monday afternoon.

5. What methods are used to hire new teachers at your school? What suggestions would you offer to improve the personnel selection process?

ISLLC Standards

STANDARD 4—A school administrator is an educational leader who promotes the success of all students by collaborating with families and community members, responding to diverse community interests and needs, and mobilizing community resources.

Knowledge

The administrator has knowledge and understanding of:

- Emerging issues and trends that potentially impact the school community
- The conditions and dynamics of the diverse school community

Dispositions

The administrator believes in, values, and is committed to:

- The proposition that diversity enriches the school
- An informed public

Performances

The administrator facilitates processes and engages in activities ensuring that:

- Information about family and community concerns, expectations, and needs is used regularly
- Diversity is recognized and valued

STANDARD 5—The school administrator is an educational leader who promotes the success of all students by acting with integrity, fairness, and in an ethical manner.

Knowledge

The administrator has knowledge and understanding of:

- The values of the diverse school community
- A professional code of ethics

Dispositions

The administrator believes in, values, and is committed to:

- Accepting the consequences for upholding one's principles and actions
- Bringing ethical principles to the decision-making process

Performances

The administrator:

- Treats people fairly, equitably, and with dignity and respect
- Demonstrates appreciation for and sensitivity to the diversity in the school community

REFERENCE

Gorton, R. A., & Schneider, G. T. (1991). *School-based leadership: Challenges and opportunities* (3rd ed.). New York: McGraw-Hill.

CASE 21

Every Day Counts

School Attendance
Is Important

Principals know that students must be in school in order for learning to take place. Every day counts by making a difference in the degree of sustained learning that occurs. Moreover, employers want to know that prospective employees have habits of dependability and punctuality. Human resource divisions of business and industry routinely review employment applications to assess attendance patterns before reviewing the same applications for academic standing. School attendance benefits society as well as individuals. Society reaps benefits from an educated and informed citizenry, while individuals are able to realize greater economic benefits because of job credentials and skills. In addition, individuals have opportunities to make more substantial contributions to their communities when their background includes educational opportunities and experiences.

Compulsory school attendance is legally governed by the concept *parens patriae,* the common law doctrine that gives the state the prerogative to secure the welfare of individuals. Because parents have a duty to educate their children, the state may compel them to do so. In the 1944 *Prince v. Massachusetts* decision, the U.S. Supreme Court found a legal guardian guilty of contributing to the delinquency of a minor by permitting her nine-year-old ward to sell Jehovah's Witnesses publications on a public street (Alexander & Alexander, 2005). The court record reads:

The family itself is not beyond regulation in the public interest . . . acting to guard the general interest in youth's well being, the state as parens partiae may restrict the parent's control by requiring school attendance, regulating or prohibiting the child's labor and in many other ways. (pp. 10–11)

This legal doctrine of *parens patriae* gives states the authority to provide for the welfare of adults and children as a "father to all persons." Because education is vital to the welfare of the state, states may require parents to send their children to school. The decision in *Prince v. Massachusetts* (1944) defined the state's prerogative as superior to parents when parents fail to provide for the welfare of their children. The court expressed the view that children have the right to be protected not only against physical abuse but also against the ignorance of parents. Heard by the U.S. Supreme Court so many years ago, this case established a precedent for attendance cases.

Decisions in cases related to school attendance are based on the beliefs that

1. Education is vital to the welfare of the state

2. The requirement of education is not an unreasonable or arbitrary exercise of state power

In most states and school districts, parents are required by statute to explain the cause of any absence of a child under their control or charge within a time period specified by school district policy. Students typically are excused for absences because of illness, death in the immediate family, inclement weather, or a valid reason preapproved by school officials.

Teachers are accountable for accurate documentation of student attendance. School attendance figures are sometimes requested for legal proceedings that center on family matters and conflicts as well as truancy cases. Beginning teachers should seek information related to regulations, policies, and required documentation about school attendance.

Local school principals who are knowledgeable about attendance requirements are able to support the work of teachers and to influence academic progress for students. While confronting parents who fail to comply with laws and regulations that govern these areas can be an unpleasant chore, benefits to students outweigh the anxiety experienced in situations that need to be remedied. In addition to knowledge of the law and local school district policies, principals must balance various factors in each individual attendance case before making a final decision. Among the factors that influence a principal's perspective are the age of the student, home life, and health.

This case involves a new principal faced with the challenge of improving attendance figures in a high school located in a suburban community adjacent to a large metropolitan area. The school has served and responded to changes in this community for 55 years. During past years, Golden Oak High School received recognition for achieving the highest rate of attendance among all high schools in the district. In more recent years, approximately 85 percent of the student population has missed 10 or more days from school each year.

As the principal, Mr. Rhodes investigates examples of poor student attendance; he has discovered that school personnel have applied local school policies with personal discretion in past years. It seems that the athletic director has favored and supported absences for varsity players, and two of the more established teachers who plan to retire are not reporting students' absences on a regular basis. Moreover, Mr. Rhodes has learned that the school counselor has played a negligible role in resolving issues of declining student achievement. Attendance problems have been addressed by homeroom teachers without input from school administrators or counselors.

FACTORS TO CONSIDER

- Administrative and teacher responsibilities for student attendance
- Adherence to school district policies by all school personnel
- Impact of student attendance on school achievement
- Use of attendance data to address student needs

THE CASE

Mr. Rhodes is a first-year principal at Golden Oak High School. The school serves 965 students in Grades 9 through 12. Students are offered many extracurricular activities, including 11 different team sports. Football is the dominant sport, supported by the community at large with a rival high school in the same district. Sports activities, in addition to 31 different clubs, present opportunities for all students to be involved in some kind of school-sponsored activity.

Most residents of the community are middle-income families, but some students live in poverty while other students are from high-income families. In the past, the student population has not been diverse, but in recent years, Hispanic and Asian families have moved to the area, creating a more diverse population. Parents work in a metropolitan area adjacent to the community. While some parents are professional people, most work for local industry or manage small businesses of their own. Most parents spend one to two hours commuting to work each day, which gives them little time to support their children's after-school activities.

The school has a reputation for having a low turnover rate among the teaching staff. Most teachers have at least 10 years of experience in their current assignments. From year to year, the school has added only one or two new teachers to the staff.

The day after his appointment by the board, Mr. Rhodes met the superintendent, Dr. Newman, on the campus at Golden Oak High School. Dr. Newman described several problems with the school's instructional program that he wanted Mr. Rhodes to improve. The most pressing concern related to school attendance. During past years, attendance had declined. Last year, Golden Oak had the lowest percentage of student attendance among all high schools in the district. Dr. Newman explained to Mr. Rhodes that school board policy was aligned with state law, which allowed excused absences only for illness, death in the immediate family, inclement weather, or a valid reason excused by the principal with prior approval. Dr. Newman also pointed out that local school district policy penalized student's grades for unexcused absences in excess of five. Upon five unexcused absences in a class, teachers had authority to subtract 10 points from the student's total number of points for the quarter. Dr. Newman also took time to describe the positive relationship between the school district and agencies such as social services and the juvenile court. He encouraged Mr. Rhodes to work closely with social services and the juvenile court system to remedy attendance problems.

The Christmas holidays had just ended, and Mr. Rhodes now turned his attention to attendance figures for the first semester. It was time to investigate the reasons for the high rate of absenteeism among selected students. As he checked the current attendance figures, he identified five of the 659 students who had missed more than 10 days during the first semester of the school year.

One of these students, Karen, was an eleventh grade student whose academic record documented grades of A's and B's during her freshman and sophomore years. Anecdotal notes included on Karen's report card reflected positive comments by teachers about the quality of her work prior to this year. She was inducted into the National Honor Society her sophomore year. The quality of Karen's work during the current year was diminished as her number of absences increased. As Mr. Rhodes checked the forms in her permanent record, he noted that she was married this past August, just before school opened. Nothing in her record indicated that the school counselor talked with her, but Mr. Rhodes found notes indicating that Karen's parents had called the counselor's office requesting conferences with teachers. Karen had missed one or two days randomly on Mondays and Fridays throughout the first semester.

Mr. Rhodes also noticed that she failed to take one of her midterm exams before Christmas.

Another student with excessive absences was named Tyrone. Tyrone, a tenth grade student in the honors program, missed 14 days during the first semester. His records reflected average progress in his classes. Two attachments to Tyrone's attendance record documented reasons for his absences. The first attachment was a handwritten excuse from his mother for an absence of five days. Tyrone's mother attended a professional conference in Washington, D.C., during September. The written excuse explained that both Tyrone and his father had accompanied her on this trip and that they toured several of the Smithsonian museums as an educational excursion. A second paper attached to Tyrone's attendance record was a typed letter signed by his dad requesting approval for Tyrone to miss another week of school in November to accompany him to Canada. Tyrone's dad explained that Tyrone had never been to Canada, and his father listed several educational reasons to justify another week's absence from school. In his note, Tyrone's dad assured the school that he would guarantee that his son would complete all missed work within a week of returning to school. Although the school district's attendance policy allowed students to miss only three days from school for personal reasons, Tyrone's homeroom teacher noted that she would excuse a second week's absence from school.

A third student, Kristina, a freshman enrolled in regular classes, missed at least four days in a row during three different weeks of the first semester. Other than these absences, Kristina was present. Form letters signed by Kristina's minister asked that she be excused from school to attend out-of-town church meetings. Specific information describing the location and dates of these meetings was not included in the letters. Kristina's homeroom teacher initialed and dated each letter and approved them as excused absences. Kristina's algebra teacher added a copy of a note requesting a conference with her parents to her permanent record folder. The algebra teacher explained that Kristina missed two major exams during the first semester due to absences. Among her grades in other academic subjects, she earned two C's and one D.

The fourth student, Carl, was in the tenth grade, and his schedule included regular classes in the morning and vocational classes in the afternoon. Carl was transported to the vocational school campus every afternoon where he received instruction in both construction trade skills and drafting. Carl's pattern of attendance reflected randomly missed days. In November, he was referred to the truant officer, who made a visit to his home. The truant office reported that Carl's parents didn't support strong attendance and told the attendance counselor that when Carl didn't feel well, he had their permission to stay home from school. The father also stated that his son's attendance was family business and not controlled by the school. The attendance counselor noted in her report that Carl's dad stated that he didn't finish high school either and that Carl could go to work with him if he wanted to instead of finishing school. Carl's personal data indicate that he had one younger brother and one younger sister enrolled, respectively, in the feeder middle and elementary schools. Mr. Rhodes made a mental note to ask the attendance counselor to check on the attendance of the younger children in Carl's family.

The fifth and final student attendance record was that of John, a junior and the quarterback on the football team. He had suffered an injury during the school district football jamboree prior to Labor Day. John was unable to play in the first two games of the season. His doctor granted permission for him to quarterback during the remainder of the season as long as he continued with physical therapy, which could only be scheduled on Tuesday and Thursday afternoons from noon until 2:30 P.M. Also in John's folder was a note from the athletic director requesting that John be excused from Friday afternoon classes to go home to rest during the football season. The athletic director had been at the school for 10 years and had coached teams to five state championships. Despite the fact that John had missed his afternoon classes three days a week, his teachers had not reported his absences as excessive.

After reviewing John's attendance record, Mr. Rhodes placed the folders of these five students on his desk. Each one presented problems that needed to be addressed. It was apparent to Mr. Rhodes that all stakeholders in the school community needed to be involved in correcting these problems and in developing a school culture that valued attendance and understood the relationship between high academic achievement and attendance.

Questions

1. What school district policies need to be reviewed with school personnel?

2. What will be the most effective way to communicate standards and expectations regarding school attendance to faculty and staff?

3. How can student achievement be linked with student attendance for professional development of teachers?

4. What should be required from students who submit form letters signed by local ministers requesting approval for absences to attend church meetings?

5. How will you propose helping school personnel other than regular classroom teachers understand the importance of and adherence to attendance policies?

Activities

1. Identify key personnel who should be involved in developing a plan to improve student attendance.

2. Outline a long-range plan to improve student attendance at Golden Oak High School.

3. Role-play a conference about approval of the second week's absence from school with Tyrone's homeroom teacher.

4. Discuss key steps in addressing each of the five different attendance cases.

5. Draft a memo to teachers explaining a process for approving student absences for reasons other than illness or emergency.

ISLLC Standards

STANDARD 1—A school administrator is an educational leader who promotes the success of all students by facilitating the development, articulation, implementation, and stewardship of a vision of learning that is shared and supported by the school community.

Knowledge

The administrator has knowledge and understanding of:

- The principles of developing and implementing strategic plans
- Information sources, data collection, and data analysis strategies

Dispositions

The administrator believes in, values, and is committed to:

- The educability of all
- Ensuring that students have the knowledge, skills, and values needed to become successful adults

Performances

The administrator facilitates processes and engages in activities ensuring that:

- Assessment data related to student learning are used to develop the school vision and goals

- Relevant demographic data pertaining to students and their families are used in developing the school mission and goals

---

STANDARD 2—A school administrator is an educational leader who promotes the success of all students by advocating, nurturing, and sustaining a school culture and instructional program conducive to student learning and staff professional growth.

Knowledge

The administrator has knowledge and understanding of:

- The change process for systems, organizations, and individuals
- School cultures

Dispositions

The administrator believes in, values, and is committed to:

- A safe and supportive learning environment
- Preparing students to be contributing members of society

Performances

The administrator facilitates processes and engages in activities ensuring that:

- Barriers to student learning are identified, clarified, and addressed
- Pupil personnel programs are developed to meet the needs of students and their families

REFERENCE

Prince v. Massachusetts, 321 U.S. 158, 64 S. Ct. 438 (1944).

CASE 22

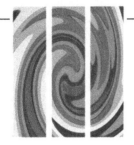

Illegal Drugs at School

Zero Tolerance Policies

Discipline is vital to classroom learning. Inappropriate or rowdy classroom behavior disrupts learning and creates an unsafe environment for the school community. As officials develop policies and procedures to address student misconduct, they should clearly define the behaviors over which the school has jurisdiction and those that outside agencies must handle.

According to Gorton and Schneider (1991), "Although schools report a wide variety of student discipline problems, they seem to fall into four general categories: (1) misbehavior in class; (2) misbehavior outside class, but in school or on school grounds; (3) truancy; and (4) tardiness" (p. 388). Behaviors that transcend what school officials are trained to handle have become a gray area in student codes of conduct. As examples, vandalism and possession of illegal drugs are serious disciplinary infractions and are also violations of law. The school's authority to determine guilt or innocence and administer punishment for those offenses is questionable. Administrators and faculty should limit themselves to defining behaviors that disrupt learning rather than actions that legal authorities will address.

The Gun-Free Schools Act of 1994, federal legislation directed at students who bring weapons to campus, introduced a new disciplinary concept to school authorities. States were mandated to enact legislation requiring at least a one-year expulsion for students who brought firearms to school. The law allowed superintendents some latitude to modify the expulsion requirements on a case-by-case basis, but the idea of zero tolerance policies was born.

Zero tolerance means that there is not an acceptable justification for a specific behavior in a given circumstance. Boards of education adopted zero tolerance policies regarding weapons in a good faith effort to improve safety in schools but have since learned that harsh, inflexible policies fail to account for a behavior's intent. In 2001, school authorities in Virginia expelled a 13-year-old boy who took a notebook that contained a knife from his friend and stored it in his locker to prevent its owner from attempting suicide. The assistant principal who discovered the weapon believed the boy was acting to protect his friend, but the district's zero tolerance weapons policy allowed no discretionary judgment. The Fourth Circuit upheld the system's policy and the child's four-month expulsion but noted the policy's harshness in its ruling (*Ratner v. Louden Co. Pub. Schools*).

Many school boards adopted similar policies regarding students' use or possession of illegal drugs on campus but quickly discovered that inflexible policy prevented administrators and teachers from using judgment when confronting student infractions. Trained police dogs and random testing of students for drugs have evolved as alternatives to the more restrictive zero tolerance policy.

The courts have handed down numerous opinions about using dogs to detect drugs on school campuses. The central question in most of the cases relates to Fourth Amendment rights regarding searches balanced against a school district's custodial responsibility for children. The Tenth Circuit allowed the use of trained police dogs to sniff lockers but did not address the constitutional issues related to illegal searches in its 2001 ruling in Texas in *Zamora v. Pomeroy*.

The Fifth Circuit, however, ruling in *U.S. v. Place* (462 U.S. 696, 1983), noted that drug-sniffing dogs are used in airports and other conveyances to enhance public safety. The Court maintained that a doctrine of "public smell" equivalent to a "plain view" doctrine for searches has evolved and noted that school officials need only "reasonable suspicion" to conduct a search and must show that the dogs are reasonably reliable in detecting contraband to justify their actions.

In continuing efforts to control drug use in schools, some districts have devised testing programs aimed at specific subgroups of students. The U.S. Supreme Court upheld a 1995 ruling in *Vernonia School District 47J v. Acton* that permitted random testing of student athletes. The Court ruled again in 2002 in *Board of Education v. Earls* that the board's policy of testing all students participating in extracurricular activities was legal because the widespread use of drugs nationally made the policy "entirely reasonable."

School administrators should be aware that no community in America is unaffected by the presence of illegal substances or their use by students. The National Center on Addiction and Substance Abuse completed a six-year study in 2001 and reported that 60% of high school students and 30% of middle school children would return that fall to schools where drugs were used, kept, or sold. The Center's report also found that 76.4% of the students who had tried marijuana (more than 1.5 million) continued its use into the twelfth grade.

Students' use of easily obtained illegal drugs looms as a major challenge for school administrators. Zero tolerance policies, drug testing, and locker and automobile searches have become common practice as officials try to educate children about the dangers of drugs. State and federal courts will have more to say about the manner in which districts attempt to cope with this problem.

FACTORS TO CONSIDER

- Case law pertaining to search and seizure on school property
- The assistant principal's role in school discipline
- Political considerations in decision making
- The effectiveness of zero tolerance policies

THE CASE

"Hey! Mr. Pinchard! We're going to win Friday night, aren't we?" Jeff asked as he retrieved two books from his locker.

Roger Pinchard smiled. The kids had been excited for two weeks about the playoff football game with DeVane High, their cross-town rival. W. H. Wilson was a slight favorite for the county championship.

"I have it on good authority that DeVane doesn't have a chance," Pinchard replied. "We'll be adding another trophy to the case at the end of the game!"

Pinchard walked through the hallway, exchanging greetings with students as he moved toward his morning duty assignment in the seniors' parking lot. The fall weather was brisk, but the assistant principal enjoyed an opportunity to go outside and leave the mounds of paperwork on his desk.

He watched from the sidewalk as students drove slowly to their parking spaces. It had taken almost one year for Roger and Ms. Morales, the principal, to devise a parking scheme for seniors. The first-come, first-served approach endorsed by the former principal had resulted in numerous accidents as students sped though the lot to park close to the building. Frequent fights and arguments had forced Ms. Morales to address the parking problem. It hadn't been easy, but peace had been restored!

Roger had been surprised by the behavior of some of the parents. He'd received telephone calls from city council members who were looking for special favors in parking lot assignments for sons and daughters of influential constituents. Even Mayor Richards had called! Thank goodness Ms. Morales had handled that one!

Dee Mathes, a cheerleader and popular senior, drove her SUV into a parking space and turned her engine off. She and three friends got out and walked toward the building.

"Morning, ladies," Pinchard said, smiling.

"Oh, hi, Mr. Pinchard," Dee said. "We're not late yet, are we?"

"No, you have 10 minutes before homeroom," he replied, looking at his watch.

As Dee passed him, Pinchard smelled the pungent aroma of marijuana.

"Dee?" he called after her.

"Yes, sir," she giggled.

"Can I talk to you for a moment?"

She motioned for her friends to continue and returned unevenly to the assistant principal.

"Are you feeling well?" Pinchard asked, moving closer to her. The odor was distinct.

Dee stepped back. "I'm fine, just excited about the game."

Pinchard nodded as Dee retreated quickly toward the building.

After the seniors were safely inside the building, Pinchard found Ms. Morales and shared his suspicion with her.

"Do you think Dee has been using drugs this morning?" the principal asked.

"The marijuana odor was strong, but I can't say for certain," Pinchard replied.

Ms. Morales shook her head. "We can't allow these kids to think that they can come to school with drugs," she said. "I'm going to call the Sheriff's office and ask him to bring his dog. We don't know if Dee and her friends were taking drugs, but we can check the cars in the student parking lot. I'll call the superintendent to tell him what we're doing."

Pinchard returned to his office. The Sheriff's deputies and their dog had visited Wilson's campus on three occasions. Ms. Morales wanted students to know that the district's zero tolerance policy for drug possession, sale, or use would be enforced at the school.

The principal appeared in Roger's doorway 30 minutes later as he completed a textbook requisition for the English department.

"The Sheriff's deputies and dog will be here in the next half-hour. I've asked the secretaries to delay any students who want to check out. You and I will meet the police in the parking lot."

"Did you call the superintendent?" Roger asked.

"He's attending a conference and couldn't be reached, but I left a message for him."

The administrators walked through the building and arrived at the parking lot to find Deputy Michaels and his dog, Alex, waiting for them.

"Good morning," the officer said. "For the record, you've requested assistance from the Sheriff's office to conduct a search of the school's parking area with Alex. Is that correct?"

Ms. Morales nodded. "Yes, I have. Mr. Pinchard thinks he smelled the odor of marijuana on one of our students this morning."

The deputy nodded and led Alex toward the first row of cars. The dog was calm until he reached Dee Mathes's SUV. He barked, stood on his hind legs, and pawed at the front-seat passenger's side window.

"I think we have something here, ma'am," Michaels said. Do you know who drove this vehicle to school?"

"I do," Pinchard said. "It belongs to a senior named Dee Mathes. I saw her arrive in it this morning."

"Is she the daughter of Roger Mathes, the city attorney?"

Ms. Morales nodded her head. "Yes, she is."

"I'm going to ask her to open her car so I can search the interior," Michaels said. "She may refuse. If she does, I'll detain her and call for a search warrant. Can you bring her to the office?"

"Yes, right away," Pinchard said, moving toward the building.

Ms. Morales waited with Deputy Michaels to call for other deputies to keep the SUV under surveillance and escorted him into the building. Dee Mathes waited nervously in the principal's office with Mr. Pinchard.

The officer asked Dee if he could search her vehicle. She agreed and accompanied him to the parking lot. Her SUV was surrounded by two police cruisers and three deputies. A group of physical education students gathered near the end of the parking lot to watch.

Deputy Michaels donned protective rubber gloves and searched the SUV's interior carefully, beginning with the driver's side. He found nothing until he moved to the front-seat passenger's side and moved a food wrapper lying on the carpet. Two marijuana cigarettes rolled from beneath the seat. He retrieved them and placed them in an evidence bag.

"Are these yours, Ms. Mathes?" he asked, turning to Dee.

"No! I've never seen them before! They aren't my drugs," she sobbed. "Am I in trouble?"

"I'm afraid so. I'm placing you under arrest for possessing an illegal substance."

A deputy stepped forward and shackled Dee's hands as he explained her constitutional rights to her. The physical education students clapped and cheered wildly from the end of the parking lot.

"We'll want to talk with the students who rode to school with Ms. Mathes," one of the deputies said. Will you call them to the office?"

"Certainly," Ms. Morales said. "We'll meet you inside in a moment."

The administrators watched as Dee was placed in a patrol car and driven off campus.

"What happens now?" Pinchard asked.

Ms. Morales walked slowly toward the building. "Several things. You can bet Dee's father will be here within the hour to protect his little girl, and we may as well start filling out the forms to recommend her expulsion from school for the rest of the year."

"Shouldn't we wait until the Sheriff tells us whether or not those were marijuana cigarettes?" Pinchard asked.

"We both know that they are," Ms. Morales replied. "We're going to have to follow the board's policy, but it's going to be tense around here for a few days."

Pinchard returned to his computer and began to write the expulsion report, but he was interrupted by his secretary.

"Mr. Pinchard, a reporter from the *Gazette* is on the phone. He has questions about the drug raid."

The assistant principal reached for his telephone, knowing the conversation wasn't going to be pleasant.

Questions

1. Did Ms. Morales and Mr. Pinchard have sufficient cause to ask police to search Dee Mathes's vehicle?

2. What should Mr. Pinchard say to the newspaper reporter?

3. Should school officials contact Dee's parents, or wait until the police do so?

4. Does your school district enforce zero tolerance policies? Are you aware of occasions on which a zero tolerance policy was inappropriate?

5. Mr. Pinchard's duties at W. H. Wilson High School are typical assignments for an assistant principal. What suggestions would you offer to prepare assistant principals more effectively for the principal's job?

Activities

1. Role-play the conference that will occur between Dee's parents and school officials.

2. What kinds of influence do you expect Dee's parents to use to resolve this case?

3. Interview a principal or assistant principal and discuss the most difficult disciplinary case they have encountered. What did they learn that might be valuable to you?

4. Interview a principal to learn what mentoring activities are used to prepare an assistant principal to meet the challenges of school leadership. How are those experiences assessed?

ISLLC Standards

STANDARD 3—A school administrator is an educational leader who promotes the success of all students by ensuring management of the organization, operations, and resources for a safe, efficient, and effective learning environment.

Knowledge

The administrator has knowledge and understanding of:

- Operational procedures at the school and district level
- Principles and issues relating to school safety and security

Dispositions

The administrator believes in, values, and is committed to:

- Making management decisions to enhance learning and teaching
- Trusting people and their judgments

Performances

The administrator facilitates processes and engages in activities ensuring that:

- Operational plans and procedures to achieve the vision and goals of the school are in place
- Potential problems and opportunities are identified

STANDARD 4—A school administrator is an educational leader who promotes the success of all students by collaborating with families and community members, responding to diverse community interests and needs, and mobilizing community resources.

Knowledge

The administrator has knowledge and understanding of:

- Emerging issues and trends that potentially impact the school community
- Community resources

Dispositions

The administrator believes in, values, and is committed to:

- Resources of the family and community needing to be brought to bear on the education of students
- An informed public

Performances

The administrator facilitates processes and engages in activities ensuring that:

- High visibility, active involvement, and communication with the larger community is a priority
- Available community resources are secured to help the school solve problems and achieve goals

REFERENCES

Board of Education v. Earls, 122 S. Ct. 2559 (2002).

Gorton, R., & Schneider, G. (1991). *School-based Leadership: Challenges and opportunities* (3rd ed.). New York: McGraw-Hill.

Gun-Free Schools Act, 1994, 20 U.S.C. (2002).

Ratner v. Louden Co. Pub. Schools, 16 Fed. Appx. 140, 143 (4th Cir., July 30, 2001).

U.S. v. Place, 462 U.S. 696 (1983).

Vernonia School District 47J v. Acton, 515 U.S. 646 (1995).

Zamora v. Pomeroy, 639 F.2d 662, 670 (10th Cir., 1981).

CASE 23

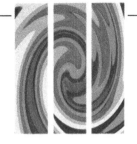

Internet Use Violations

Threats Over the
World Wide Web

The very first homework assignment new administrators and teachers should complete is to read and become familiar with school board policies, particularly those that apply to student behavior. All educators have a significant responsibility to appropriately resolve situations that require disciplinary action.

A new dimension of violations that principals must handle has developed. A category of disciplinary incidents that has suddenly gained increasing attention is that of Internet offenses. These incidents range from improper use of the Internet by students while at school to criticism of school personnel on Web sites designed by students using home computers. Legal guidance available to school personnel is inconclusive because "courts have not spoken with a single voice on the First Amendment issues raised in these cases" (Cambron-McCabe, McCarthy, & Thomas, 2004, p. 124).

A significant decision of the U.S. Supreme Court in *Reno v. American Civil Liberties Union* (1997) assigns First Amendment protection to the Internet categorizing Internet communications as more like print than broadcast media. The decision in the *Reno* case may have been a reaction to the Communications Decency Act (CDA) enacted by Congress in 1996, which "sought to control 'cyberporn' and, thereby, protect minors from harmful material on the Internet . . . the U.S. Supreme Court held the Act to be unconstitutional because it was 'facially overbroad' in violation of the First Amendment" (Alexander & Alexander, 2005, p. 397). The majority opinion in this case reasoned "that under the law as now written a parent could face a lengthy prison term for sending her seventeen-year-old college freshman daughter information about birth control by e-mail" (Alexander & Alexander, p. 397).

The 1998 case *Beussink v. Woodland R-IV School District* communicated to educators that a student-created homepage may fall under First Amendment protection. Brandon Beussink, who was a senior at Woodland High School, created a homepage that displayed inappropriate language for a school setting and that criticized the school. Amanda Brown, a friend of Brandon Beussink, used his computer while visiting his home, and Brandon allowed her to access the offensive Web site. Sometime later Amanda and Brandon had a disagreement, and Amanda used the Web site to exact revenge against Brandon. Amanda accessed the Web site while at school and showed it to the computer teacher at Woodland High.

When the computer teacher reported this incident to the principal, Mr. Poorman, Mr. Poorman immediately viewed the Web page and decided to suspend Brandon for five days, which he later increased to 10 days. The U.S. District Court of the Eastern District of Missouri concluded that information posted on the offensive Web page was constitutionally protected speech because there was no evidence that disruption occurred either in the library or classrooms of the school. The court ruled that "Disliking or being upset by the content of the student's speech is not an acceptable justification for limiting student speech under *Tinker*" (*Beussink v. Woodland R-IV School District*, 1998).

In *Emmett v. Kent School District* (2000), a federal district court found for a student suspended for five days when he created Web pages featuring mock obituaries of students. The student included a place for those who visited the site to vote on which one of the students listed on the site should die next. A television station found out about and reported on the Web page, referring to the list of students as a "hit list." After the news report, the student removed the Web page. School officials first expelled the student on an emergency basis; later the expulsion was changed to a five-day suspension. Deciding in favor of the student, the court reasoned that "the student's web site was not produced in connection with any class or school activity, and school personnel failed to substantiate that the material threatened or intended harm to anyone" (*Emmett v. Kent School District*, 2000).

In a more recent case, *Killion v. Franklin Regional School District* (2001), a student e-mailed critical and disparaging remarks about a teacher to his friends. Because the student used his home computer and did not make copies available to other students at school, the court ruled that the student's e-mail was protected speech under the First Amendment and invalidated his suspension from school.

In order to provide parameters for use of the Internet at school, school boards have developed Acceptable Use Policies. Typical provisions of such policies include definitions of technological terms, purpose of Internet use, rights and responsibilities of a school district, examples of acceptable use, examples of unacceptable use, and consequences of unacceptable use. From the perspective of a school district, acceptable use of the Internet is to support research and instruction. Acceptable use of the Internet at school includes using appropriate language, respecting the copyright law and license agreements, and using online time efficiently. Unacceptable use of the Internet at school includes activities such as transmitting threatening or obscene material, downloading lewd or indecent text or graphics, and willfully spreading computer viruses.

The following case requires a principal to deal with a situation in which a student has offended and possibly threatened a teacher through a Web page created at home on his or her personal computer. The principal will be required to balance the free speech rights of the student against the rights of the school district to maintain a productive and safe school environment.

FACTORS TO CONSIDER

- First Amendment free speech rights of students
- Application of Acceptable Use Policies
- Communication with parents and students
- Public relations

THE CASE

Roosevelt High School is in an affluent area of a large city. This section of the city has always been an affluent area in which families have secure financial means. Parents are professionals such as doctors, lawyers, or partners in investment firms. Residential areas feature large lots on low rolling hills of manicured lawns and stately homes. Because of the secure financial circumstances of families, students in this community have the latest fashion in clothes and the newest technology available to them.

Dr. Steven Forbes has been principal of Roosevelt High School for nine years. He was recognized as Principal of the Year by the state secondary principals' association two years ago. He is an established principal, respected by parents, and focused on maintaining a reputation as principal of the most prestigious school in the state. Dr. Forbes is proud of the highly regarded reputation of his school. He has worked diligently to recommend only the most highly qualified teacher applicants for available positions. Among the newest teacher appointees is Miss Cindy Walker. Dr. Forbes hired Miss Walker one year ago to teach specialized science courses such as zoology, botany, and genetics.

When hired to teach at Roosevelt High School, Miss Walker was a beginning teacher. Because she had completed her undergraduate degree, master's degree, and another year of postgraduate work before applying for a teaching position, she was a little older than most beginning teachers. Miss Walker has never married, and she is intent on establishing a structured classroom focused on academics. The rigor of the subjects she is assigned to teach, combined with her serious approach to instructional delivery, establishes a classroom in which students experience high levels of stress. Dr. Forbes has received numerous calls about Miss Walker's stringent expectations from parents concerned that their children will make their first low grade in high school. Many students in Miss Walker's classes aspire to be valedictorian or salutatorian, which generates intense competition for the highest grades in their classes. Although Dr. Forbes has discussed techniques Miss Walker can use to reduce student stress and increase positive interactions with students, she hasn't successfully implemented his suggestions. Parents and students continue to complain about the class workload and poor instruction.

In November of Miss Walker's second year at Roosevelt High School, the Veteran's Day holiday fell on a Friday and provided a long weekend for students and school personnel. Miss Walker took advantage of the three-day weekend to drive three hours one-way to visit with her parents. When she returned to her apartment on Sunday afternoon, she checked her e-mail messages and found an unidentified one that urged her to view a specific Web site for a personal message. Curious, she logged on to the Web site and was horrified to find highly suggestive comments about her personal behaviors and critical comments about the rigor of her classes using vulgar curse words. The final comment on the Web site was, "Who wants Miss Walker to disappear?"

Miss Walker rushed to the telephone and tearfully called Dr. Forbes, reporting, "They've threatened to kill me, Dr. Forbes. What am I to do? I may not be safe alone in my apartment tonight!"

"Calm down, Miss Walker, and speak slowly. I need to clearly understand what you're talking about."

"It's a Web page, Dr. Forbes! Someone created a Web page that suggests someone kill me! Should I call the police?"

"Well, I don't know, Miss Walker. Can you give me the URL for the Web page? Once I see what you're talking about, I'll know better how to help you."

Miss Walker forwarded the e-mail to Dr. Forbes. He logged on, read the e-mail, and clicked on the link to the threatening Web page. Once he read the e-mail and saw the Web page, he immediately called Miss Walker. "I can understand your concern, Miss Walker, but I sincerely believe the e-mail and Web page are a prank. Is there a student who is unhappy with you? Think about last week and try to remember particular incidents with disgruntled or disruptive students."

"I'll bet that Randy Franks did this, Dr. Forbes. He doesn't like me and makes snide comments to other students whenever I turn my back to the class. He's so clever that I haven't been able to prove that he's the disruptive influence, but I'll just bet Randy developed this Web page. The other students ask for his help with computer problems all the time."

"I'm going to print hard copies of the e-mail and Web page, Miss Walker. In the morning, you and I will need to speak with Randy and some of his friends who may know if he developed this Web site. If necessary, we'll ask the district technologist to help us determine where the e-mail originated."

"Thanks, Dr. Forbes. I'll see you in the morning. If you need to reach me tonight, please call my mom's house. I'm going to spend the night with my parents."

Questions

1. What policies apply to this situation?

2. Who needs to be involved in resolving this situation?

3. How should Dr. Forbes and Miss Walker proceed with determining the source of the e-mail and creator of the Web site? How should this case be approached if comments about the teacher were written in an anonymous note rather than posted on a Web site?

4. When the student(s) who sent the e-mail and created the Web page are identified, should Dr. Forbes assign disciplinary consequences? If so, how severe should the consequences be?

5. What can school officials do to minimize misuse of the Internet?

Activities

1. Develop a draft of an Acceptable Use Policy.

2. List different consequences that could be considered for unacceptable on-campus use of the Internet and for off-campus use of the Internet that disrupts the school.

3. Role-play a conference with parents of the student who was determined to have sent the e-mail and developed the Web site.

4. Prepare an outline of points about use of the Internet by students and teachers to discuss during a faculty meeting. Identify aspects of your state's school laws that are related to issues presented in this case.

5. Role-play a conference between Dr. Forbes and Randy Franks.

ISLLC Standards

STANDARD 5—A school administrator is an educational leader who promotes the success of all students by acting with integrity, fairness, and in an ethical manner.

Knowledge

The administrator has knowledge and understanding of:

- The purpose of education and the role of leadership in modern society
- Various ethical frameworks and perspectives on ethics

Dispositions

- The principles in the Bill of Rights
- Development of a caring school community

Performances

- Protects the rights and confidentiality of students and staff
- Fulfills legal and contractual obligations

STANDARD 6—A school administrator is an educational leader who promotes the success of all students by understanding, responding to, and influencing the larger political, social, economic, legal, and cultural context.

Knowledge

The administrator has knowledge and understanding of:

- The law as related to education and schooling
- Social, cultural, and economic contexts of schooling

Dispositions

The administrator believes in, values, and is committed to:

- The importance of a continuing dialogue with other decision makers affecting education
- Use of legal systems to protect student rights and improve student opportunities

Performances

The administrator facilitates processes and engages in activities ensuring that:

- The environment in which schools operate is influenced on behalf of students and their families
- Communication occurs among the school community concerning trends, issues, and potential changes in the environment in which schools operate

REFERENCES

Alexander, K., & Alexander, D. (2005). *American public school law* (6th ed.). Belmont, CA: Wadsworth.

Beussink v. Woodland R-IV School District, 30 F. Supp. 2d 1175 (E.D. Mo. 1998).

Cambron-McCabe, N. H., McCarthy, M. M., & Thomas, S. B. (2004). *Public school law* (5th ed.). Boston: Pearson Education.

Emmett v. Kent School District No. 415, 92 F. Supp. 2d 446 (2001).

Killion v. Franklin Regional School District, 136 F. Supp. 2d 446 (2001).

Reno v. American Civil Liberties Union, 521 U.S. 844, 117 S. Ct. 2329 (1997).

Bibliography

Alexander, K., & Alexander, M. (2005). *American public school law* (6th ed.). Belmont, CA: Thomson West.

Beussink v. Woodland R-IV School District, 30 F. Supp. 2d 1175 (E.D. Mo. 1998).

Board of Education v. Earls, 122 S. Ct. 2559 (2002).

Board of Education v. Wood, 717 S.W.2d 837 (Ky. 1986).

Cambron-McCabe, N. H., McCarthy, M. M., & Thomas, S. B. (2004). *Public school law* (5th ed.). Boston: Pearson Education.

Commonwealth v. Cass, 709 A.2d 350 (Pa. 1998).

Drake, T. L., & Roe, W. H. *The principalship* (6th ed.). Upper Saddle River, NJ: Merrill-Prentice Hall.

DuFour, R., DuFour, R., Eaker, R., & Karhanek, G. (2004). *Whatever it takes.* Bloomington, IN: National Educational Service.

Emmett v. Kent School District No. 415, 92 F. Supp. 2d 446 (2000).

Enghagen, L. K. (1997). *Fair use guidelines for educators.* Northampton, MA: Sterling Publications.

Gordon, E. W., Bridglall, B. L., & Meroe, A. S. (2004). *Supplementary education: The hidden curriculum of high academic achievement.* Lanham, MD: Rowman & Littlefield Publishers. (ERIC Document Reproduction Service No. ED489047)

Gorton, R. A., & Schneider, G. T. (1991). *School-based leadership: Challenges and opportunities* (3rd ed.). New York: McGraw-Hill.

Gun-Free Schools Act, 1994, 20 U.S.C. (2002).

The Individuals With Disabilities Act (Pub. L. No 101-476), 5 (b) (4), 1991.

In Re: Donna Thomas, Board of Education of Cape Girardeau School District No. 63, v. Donna Thomas, 926 S.W. 2d 163 (Mo. E.D. Div. Two 1996).

International Baccalaureate Program. (2005, November 20). *IB diploma program.* Retrieved June 19, 2006, from http://www.ebu1.org/main/Academic program/IB/ib.html

Killion v. Franklin Regional School District, 136 F. Supp. 2d 446 (2001).

Kuehn v. Reston School District No. 403, 103 Wash. 2d 594, 694 P.2d 1078 (1985).

Lunenburg, F. C. (1995). *The principalship: Concepts and applications.* Upper Saddle River, NJ: Merrill-Prentice Hall.

Marsh, C. J., & Willis, G. (2003). *Curriculum: Alternative approaches, ongoing issues* (3rd ed.). Upper Saddle River, NJ: Pearson Education.

Matthews, L. J., & Crow, G. M. (2003). *Being and becoming a principal: Role conceptions for contemporary principals and assistant principals.* Boston: Pearson Education.

New Jersey v. T.L.O., 469 U.S. 325, 342 n. 8 (1985).

Oliva, P. F., & Pawlas, G. E. (2004). *Supervision for today's schools* (7th ed.). Hoboken, NJ: Wiley/Jossey-Bass.

Owens, R. F. (1998). *Organizational behavior in education* (6th ed.). Boston: Allyn & Bacon.

Prince v. Massachusetts, 321 U.S. 158, 64 S. Ct. 438 (1944).

Ratner v. Louden Co. Pub. Schools, 16 Fed. Appx. 140, 143 (4th Cir., July 30, 2001).

Reno v. American Civil Liberties Union, 521 U.S. 844, 117 S. Ct. 2329 (1997).

Rowland v. Mad River Local School District, 730 F.2d 444 (6th Cir. 1984).

Smith, W., & Andrews, R. (1989). *Instructional leadership: How principals make a difference.* Alexandria, VA: Association for Supervision and Curriculum Development.

Stader, D. L. (2007). *Law and ethics in educational leadership.* Upper Saddle River, NJ: Pearson Education.

Ubben, G. C., & Hughes, L. W. (1997). *The principal: Creative leadership for effective schools.* Boston: Allyn & Bacon.

Ubben, G. C., Hughes, L. W., & Norris, C. J. (2004). *The principal: Creative leadership for excellence in schools* (5th ed.). Boston: Pearson Education.

U.S. v. Place, 462 U.S. 696 (1983).

Vernonia School District 47J v. Acton, 515 U.S. 646 (1995).

Wiles, J., & Bondi, J. (1996). *Supervision: A guide to practice* (4th ed.). Upper Saddle River, NJ: Prentice Hall.

Wiles, J., & Bondi, J. (2002). *Curriculum development: A guide to practice.* Upper Saddle River, NJ: Merrill-Prentice Hall.

Zamora v. Pomeroy, 639 F.2d 662, 670 (10th Cir. 1981).

Appendix A

ISLLC Standards

STANDARD 1—A school administrator is an educational leader who promotes the success of all students by facilitating the development, articulation, implementation, and stewardship of a vision of learning that is shared and supported by the school community.

Knowledge

The administrator has knowledge and understanding of:
- Learning goals in a pluralistic society
- The principles of developing and implementing strategic plans
- Systems theory
- Information sources, data collection, and data analysis strategies
- Effective communication
- Effective consensus-building and negotiation skills

Dispositions

The administrator believes in, values, and is committed to:
- The educability of all
- A school vision of high standards of learning
- Continuous school improvement
- The inclusion of all members of the school community
- Ensuring that students have the knowledge, skills, and values needed to become successful adults
- A willingness to continuously examine one's own assumptions, beliefs, and practices
- Doing the work required for high levels of personal and organization performance

Performances

The administrator facilitates processes and engages in activities ensuring that:

- The vision and mission of the school are effectively communicated to staff, parents, students, and community members
- The vision and mission are communicated through the use of symbols, ceremonies, stories, and similar activities
- The core beliefs of the school vision are modeled for all stakeholders
- The vision is developed with and among stakeholders
- The contributions of school community members to the realization of the vision are recognized and celebrated
- Progress toward the vision and mission is communicated to all stakeholders
- The school community is involved in school improvement efforts
- The vision shapes the educational programs, plans, and activities
- The vision shapes the educational programs, plans, and actions
- An implementation plan is developed in which objectives and strategies to achieve the vision and goals are clearly articulated
- Assessment data related to student learning are used to develop the school vision and goals
- Relevant demographic data pertaining to students and their families are used in developing the school mission and goals
- Barriers to achieving the vision are identified, clarified, and addressed
- Needed resources are sought and obtained to support the implementation of the school mission and goals
- Existing resources are used in support of the school vision and goals
- The vision, mission, and implementation plans are regularly monitored, evaluated, and revised

---

STANDARD 2—A school administrator is an educational leader who promotes the success of all students by advocating, nurturing, and sustaining a school culture and instructional program conducive to student learning and staff professional growth.

Knowledge

The administrator has knowledge and understanding of:

- Student growth and development
- Applied learning theories
- Applied motivational theories
- Curriculum design, implementation, evaluation, and refinement
- Principles of effective instruction

- Measurement, evaluation, and assessment strategies
- Diversity and its meaning for educational programs
- Adult learning and professional development models
- The change process for systems, organizations, and individuals
- The role of technology in promoting student learning and professional growth
- School cultures

Dispositions

The administrator believes in, values, and is committed to:

- Student learning as the fundamental purpose of schooling
- The proposition that all students can learn
- The variety of ways in which students can learn
- Life-long learning for self and others
- Professional development as an integral part of school improvement
- The benefits that diversity brings to the school community
- A safe and supportive learning environment
- Preparing students to be contributing members of society

Performances

The administrator facilitates processes and engages in activities ensuring that:

- All individuals are treated with fairness, dignity, and respect
- Professional development promotes a focus on student learning consistent with the school vision and goals
- Students and staff feel valued and important
- The responsibilities and contributions of each individual are acknowledged
- Barriers to student learning are identified, clarified, and addressed
- Diversity is considered in developing learning experiences
- Life-long learning is encouraged and modeled
- There is a culture of high expectations for self, student, and staff performance
- Technologies are used in teaching and learning
- Student and staff accomplishments are recognized and celebrated
- Multiple opportunities to learn are available to all students
- The school is organized and aligned for success
- Curricular, co-curricular, and extracurricular programs are designed, implemented, evaluated, and refined
- Curriculum decisions are based on research, expertise of teachers, and the recommendations of learned societies
- The school culture and climate are assessed on a regular basis

- A variety of sources of information is used to make decisions
- Student learning is assessed using a variety of techniques
- Multiple sources of information regarding performance are used by staff and students
- A variety of supervisory and evaluation models is employed
- Pupil personnel programs are developed to meet the needs of students and their families

---

STANDARD 3—A school administrator is an educational leader who promotes the success of all students by ensuring management of the organization, operations, and resources for a safe, efficient, and effective learning environment.

Knowledge

The administrator has knowledge and understanding of:

- Theories and models of organizations and the principles of organizational development
- Operational procedures at the school and district level
- Principles and issues relating to school safety and security
- Human resources management and development
- Principles and issues relating to fiscal operations of school management
- Principles and issues relating to school facilities and use of space
- Legal issues impacting school operations
- Current technologies that support management functions

Dispositions

The administrator believes in, values, and is committed to:

- Making management decisions to enhance learning and teaching
- Taking risks to improve schools
- Trusting people and their judgments
- Accepting responsibility
- High-quality standards, expectations, and performances
- Involving stakeholders in management processes
- A safe environment

Performances

The administrator facilitates processes and engages in activities ensuring that:

- Knowledge of learning, teaching, and student development is used to inform management decisions

- Operational procedures are designed and managed to maximize opportunities for successful learning
- Emerging trends are recognized, studied, and applied as appropriate
- Operational plans and procedures to achieve the vision and goals of the school are in place
- Collective bargaining and other contractual agreements related to the school are effectively managed
- The school plant, equipment, and support systems operate safely, efficiently, and effectively
- Time is managed to maximize attainment of organizational goals
- Potential problems and opportunities are identified
- Problems are confronted and resolved in a timely manner
- Financial, human, and material resources are aligned to the goals of schools
- The school acts entrepreneurially to support continuous improvement
- Organizational systems are regularly monitored and modified as needed
- Stakeholders are involved in decisions affecting schools
- Responsibility is shared to maximize ownership and accountability
- Effective problem-framing and problem-solving skills are used
- Effective conflict resolution skills are used
- Effective group-process and consensus-building skills are used
- Effective communication skills are used
- There is effective use of technology to manage school operations
- Fiscal resources of the school are managed responsibly, efficiently, and effectively
- A safe, clean, and aesthetically pleasing school environment is created and maintained
- Human resource functions support the attainment of school goals
- Confidentiality and privacy of school records are maintained

---

STANDARD 4—A school administrator is an educational leader who promotes the success of all students by collaborating with families and community members, responding to diverse community interests and needs, and mobilizing community resources.

Knowledge

The administrator has knowledge and understanding of:

- Emerging issues and trends that potentially impact the school community
- The conditions and dynamics of the diverse school community

- Community resources
- Community relations and marketing strategies and processes
- Successful models of school, family, business, community, government and higher education partnerships

Dispositions

The administrator believes in, values, and is committed to:
- Schools operating as an integral part of the larger community
- Collaboration and communication with families
- Involvement of families and other stakeholders in school decision-making processes
- The proposition that diversity enriches the school
- Families as partners in the education of their children
- The proposition that families have the best interests of their children in mind
- Resources of the family and community needing to be brought to bear on the education of students
- An informed public

Performances

The administrator facilitates processes and engages in activities ensuring that:
- High visibility, active involvement, and communication with the larger community is a priority
- Relationships with community leaders are identified and nurtured
- Information about family and community concerns, expectations, and needs is used regularly
- There is outreach to different business, religious, political, and service agencies and organizations
- Credence is given to individuals and groups whose values and opinions may conflict
- The school and community serve one another as resources
- Available community resources are secured to help the school solve problems and achieve goals
- Partnerships are established with area businesses, institutions of higher education, and community groups to strengthen programs and support school goals
- Community youth family services are integrated with school programs
- Community stakeholders are treated equitably
- Diversity is recognized and valued
- Effective media relations are developed and maintained
- A comprehensive program of community relations is established

- Public resources and funds are used appropriately and wisely
- Community collaboration is modeled for staff
- Opportunities for staff to develop collaborative skills are provided

---

STANDARD 5—A school administrator is an educational leader who promotes the success of all students by acting with integrity, fairness, and in an ethical manner.

Knowledge

The administrator has knowledge and understanding of:

- The purpose of education and the role of leadership in modern society
- Various ethical frameworks and perspectives on ethics
- The values of the diverse school community
- Professional codes of ethics
- The philosophy and history of education

Dispositions

The administrator believes in, values, and is committed to:

- The ideal of the common good
- The principles in the Bill of Rights
- The right of every student to a free, quality education
- Bringing ethical principles to the decision-making process
- Subordinating one's own interest to the good of the school community
- Accepting the consequences for upholding one's principles and actions
- Using the influence of one's office constructively and productively in the service of all students and their families
- Development of a caring school community

Performances

The administrator:

- Examines personal and professional values
- Demonstrates a personal and professional code of ethics
- Demonstrates values, beliefs, and attitudes that inspire others to higher levels of performance
- Serves as a role model
- Accepts responsibility for school operations
- Considers the impact of one's administrative practices on others
- Uses the influence of the office to enhance the educational program rather than for personal gain

- Treats people fairly, equitably, and with dignity and respect
- Protects the rights and confidentiality of students and staff
- Demonstrates appreciation for and sensitivity to the diversity in the school community
- Recognizes and respects the legitimate authority of others
- Examines and considers the prevailing values of the diverse school community
- Expects that others in the school community will demonstrate integrity and exercise ethical behavior
- Opens the school to public scrutiny
- Fulfills legal and contractual obligations
- Applies laws and procedures fairly, wisely, and considerately

---

STANDARD 6—A school administrator is an educational leader who promotes the success of all students by understanding, responding to, and influencing the larger political, social, economic, legal, and cultural context.

Knowledge

The administrator has knowledge and understanding of:

- Principles of representative governance that undergird the system of American schools
- The role of public education in developing and renewing a democratic society and an economically productive nation
- The law as related to education and schooling
- The political, social, cultural, and economic systems and processes that impact schools
- Models and strategies of change and conflict resolution as applied to the larger political, social, cultural, and economic contexts of schooling
- Global issues and forces affecting teaching and learning
- The dynamics of policy development and advocacy under our democratic political system
- The importance of diversity and equity in a democratic society

Dispositions

The administrator believes in, values, and is committed to:

- Education as a key to opportunity and social mobility
- Recognizing a variety of ideas, values, and cultures

- Importance of a continuing dialogue with other decision makers affecting education
- Actively participating in the political and policy-making context in the service of education
- Using legal systems to protect student rights and improve student opportunities

Performances

The administrator facilitates processes and engages in activities ensuring that:

- The environment in which schools operate is influenced on behalf of students and their families
- Communication occurs among the school community concerning trends, issues, and potential changes in the environment in which schools operate
- There is ongoing dialogue with representatives of diverse community groups
- The school community works within the framework of policies, laws, and regulations enacted by local, state, and federal authorities
- Public policy is shaped to provide quality education for students
- Lines of communication are developed with decision makers outside the school community

SOURCE: The ISLLC Standards for School Leaders are reprinted by permission. The Interstate School Leaders Licensure Consortium Standards were developed by the Council of Chief State School Officers (CCSSO) and member states. Copies may be downloaded from the Council's Web site at www.ccsso.org. Council of Chief State School Officers, 1996, *Interstate School Leaders Licensure Consortium (ISLLC) standards for school leaders*. Washington, DC: Author.

Appendix B

Annotated Suggested Readings

Beckner, E. (2004). *Ethics for educational leaders*. Boston: Pearson Education.

School leaders are required to make numerous decisions daily. This book blends educational philosophy and theory to support practical solutions to complex problems.

Bolman, L. G., & Deal, T. E. (2002). *Reframing the path to school leadership*. Thousand Oaks, CA: Corwin Press.

Novice and experienced educators interact in mentoring scenarios using four different frames to address conflicts and problems in *Reframing the Path to School Leadership*. Lee Bolman and Terrence Deal illustrate how teachers and principals gain insight and professional growth through the political, human resource, structural, and symbolic frames of viewing professional challenges.

Bolman, L. G., & Deal, T. E. (2006). *The wizard and the warrior: Leading with passion and power*. San Francisco: Jossey-Bass.

Lee Bolman and Terrence Deal describe leadership through the roles of the wizard and the warrior, two distinctly different characters. While the wizard leader depends on creativity and imagination to succeed, the warrior leader exercises courage and personal strength to realize success. Applying characteristics of these two roles with flexible force results in confident leadership.

Brubaker, D. L. (1994). *Creative curriculum leadership*. Thousand Oaks, CA: Corwin Press.

Dale Brubaker presents a formula for using spiritual and political power to nurture creative curriculum leadership. Through real-life examples, he illustrates how educators can cultivate learning communities.

Collins, J. (2001). *Good to great*. New York: HarperCollins.

Good to Great presents conclusions analyzed by Jim Collins and his research team of differences between companies known to be highly successful and companies recognized as good but never great. Results present the reader with insight into effective leadership and management practices.

Covey, S. R. (1990). *Principle-centered leadership*. New York: Fireside, Simon & Schuster.

In *Principle-Centered Leadership,* Stephen Covey presents principles on which effective leaders build meaningful personal and professional relationships. He guides the reader to achieve balance that results in higher productivity and greater personal satisfaction.

Dickman, M. H., & Stanford-Blair, N. (2002). *Connecting leadership to the brain*. Thousand Oaks, CA: Corwin Press.

Michael Dickman and Nancy Stanford-Blair connect effective leadership practices with the most current findings about how the brain processes information and learns. The authors offer readers reflective exercises for applying *mindful* leadership.

DuFour, R., DuFour, R., Eaker, R., & Karhanek, G. (2004). *Whatever it takes*. Bloomington, IN: National Educational Service.

Richard DuFour and his colleagues describe how committed educators support the learning of all students. The characteristics of professional learning communities are illustrated as theory is transformed into practice in four different schools.

English, F. W. (1992). *Deciding what to teach and test*. Newbury Park, CA: Corwin Press.

In *Deciding What to Teach and Test,* Fenwick English distinguishes among the formal, informal, and hidden versions of curriculum. He presents a structured approach to evaluating a school's curriculum and aligning what is taught with what is tested.

Glatthorn, A. A. (1997). *The principal as curriculum leader: Shaping what is taught and tested.* Thousand Oaks, CA: Corwin Press.

In *The Principal as Curriculum Leader: Shaping What Is Taught and Tested,* Allan Glatthorn presents four different levels of curriculum shaped by the state, the district, the local school, and the individual classroom. He connects the role of an effective leader with curriculum formed at each of the four levels.

Glickman, C. D. (2002). *Leadership for learning.* Alexandria, VA: Association for Supervision and Curriculum Development.

Carl Glickman shows instructional leaders how to conduct observations and work collaboratively with teachers. He presents formats for supporting classroom instruction that lead to total school improvement.

Goleman, D., Boyatzis, R., & McKee, A. (2002). *Primal leadership: Learning to lead with emotional intelligence.* Boston: Harvard Business School Press.

In *Primal Leadership: Learning to Lead With Emotional Intelligence,* Daniel Goleman and his colleagues Richard Boyatzis and Annie McKee emphasize the impact a leader's emotions have on the culture of an organization. The authors illustrate how important it is for leaders to build positive relationships with others.

Green, R. L. (2005). *Practicing the art of leadership: A problem-based approach to implementing the ISLLC standards* (2nd ed.). Upper Saddle River, NJ: Pearson Education.

Reginald Green uses the five areas of decision making, communication, change, conflict management, and establishment of an effective teaching and learning climate to illustrate a process of developing leadership behaviors that produces results and meets standards of accountability. He presents situations supported by theory that achieve standards of accountability.

Lambert, L. (1998). *Building leadership capacity in schools*. Alexandria, VA: Association for Supervision and Curriculum Development.

Building Leadership Capacity in Schools is a plan for schools and school districts to develop and maintain effective school leadership. Linda Lambert illustrates five characteristics of effective leadership that results in increased student learning as she tells the stories of three schools.

Lambert, L. (2003). *Leadership capacity for lasting school improvement*. Alexandria, VA: Association for Supervision and Curriculum Development.

Linda Lambert builds on her previous work, *Building Leadership Capacity in Schools,* to investigate ways for school leaders to assess and enhance their leadership skills.

Marzano, R. J., Waters, T., & McNulty, B. A. (2005). *School leadership that works: From research to results*. Alexandria, VA: Association for Supervision and Curriculum Development.

Robert Marzano and his colleagues Timothy Waters and Brian McNulty present an analysis of studies of school leadership that positively affects student achievement. The authors present the reader with 21 "leadership responsibilities" that support increased student achievement.

National Association of Elementary School Principals. (2004). *Leading learning communities: Standards for what principals should know and be able to do* (3rd ed.). Alexandria, VA: Author.

In *Leading Learning Communities: Standards for What Principals Should Know and Be Able to Do,* the National Association of Elementary School Principals (NAESP) presents six standards that describe instructional school leadership. Emphasis is placed on developing a culture of learning for adults as well as students.

Reeves, D. B. (2006). *The learning leader: How to focus school improvement for better results*. Alexandria, VA: Association for Supervision and Curriculum Development.

Douglas Reeves extends student achievement to factors other than test results. He offers an outline of *leadership for learning* that is directed by a leadership team focused on the importance of converting research conclusions into student success.

Sernak, K. (1998). *School leadership: Balancing power with caring.* New York: Teachers College Press.

How one principal weaves authority with a caring attitude to create a positive school culture is examined in a school with a history of numerous student problems with drugs and violence. Kathy Sernak describes how authority, power, and a caring attitude blend to create a culture of reform and progress.

Smith, W. F., & Andrews, R. L. (1989). *Instructional leadership: How principals make a difference.* Alexandria, VA: Association for Supervision and Curriculum Development.

Wilma Smith and Richard Andrews guide the reader in developing *moral, ethical,* and *legal* practices that result in schools that are organized to help students achieve to their full potential. The authors describe how different leadership styles can result in instructional leadership that leads to increased student achievement.

Stader, D. L. (2007). *Law and ethics in educational leadership.* Upper Saddle River, NJ: Pearson Education.

The book *Law and Ethics in Educational Leadership* offers the reader practical guidance for how to and how not to address school problems. The legal foundations of education are blended with ethical principles and aligned with both Educational Leadership Constituent Council (ELCC) and ISLLC standards to guide the work of school leaders.

Zmuda, A., Kuklis, R., & Kline, E. (2004). *Transforming schools: Creating a culture of continuous improvement.* Alexandria, VA: Association for Supervision and Curriculum Development.

Concepts of continuous school improvement and systems thinking are emphasized as processes for building productive staff development programs. Instructional leaders are given a model for using data to bridge the gap between current scores and future academic growth and improvement.

Index

About the Authors

David L. Gray is Associate Professor of Instructional Leadership and Chair of the Department of Leadership and Teacher Education at the University of South Alabama in Mobile, Alabama. He received his Ed.D. in Leadership and Supervision from the University of Alabama and his M.Ed. in Administration and Supervision from Frostburg State University in Frostburg, Maryland. He served as a teacher, assistant principal, and principal for 23 years before accepting his present position. He has been at the University of South Alabama since 1997.

He has published numerous articles that address the principal's responsibilities for professional development, teacher recruiting and retention, and using data to make decisions in schools. His research interests focus on inclusive classrooms and teacher preparation programs. He teaches courses that center on the supervisory practices of instructional leaders and instructional leadership and curriculum development. He resides with his wife and three sons in Spanish Fort, Alabama. Author of *The Fourth Seal,* he will publish a second novel in 2007.

Agnes E. Smith is Associate Professor of Educational Leadership at the University of South Alabama. She received the Ed.D. in Educational Leadership from Auburn University and the M.Ed. in Elementary Education from the University of Louisiana at Monroe. Dr. Smith's professional experience includes elementary teaching of Grades 2 through 5, assistant instructional leadership positions, and principal at the K–8 levels of education. She has been at the University of South Alabama since 1997.

In 1992, she was named Alabama PTA Secondary Principal of the Year. She currently serves as a State Specialist for the Southern Association of Colleges and Schools working with schools toward initial and continued accreditation following the *Quality Assurance* school improvement process. She teaches courses in educational leadership that focus on legal and ethical dimensions of school leadership and mentoring for professional growth and development. She presents papers at national and state conferences and in local schools on topics such as professionalism and building community relationships that make a difference. Her research interests include mentoring leadership and school leadership preparation programs. She has published articles on qualities of effective leadership and on conducting interviews with prospective teachers. She serves as coeditor of an effective teacher resource guide for professional growth and development. She presents papers at national and state conferences and in local schools on topics such as professionalism and building community relationships that make a difference. Her research interests include mentoring leadership and school leadership preparation programs. She has published articles on qualities of effective leadership and on conducting interviews with prospective teachers. She serves as coeditor of an effective teacher resource guide.

Lightning Source UK Ltd.
Milton Keynes UK
UKHW031815120321
380242UK00003B/8